COYOTE'S COUNCIL FIRE

COYOTE'S COUNCIL FIRE

CONTEMPORARY SHAMANS ON RACE, GENDER, & COMMUNITY

LOREN CRUDEN

Destiny Books
Rochester, Vermont

Destiny Books
One Park Street
Rochester, Vermont 05767

LIBRARY OF CONGRESS CATALOGING-IN-PUBLICATION DATA
Cruden, Loren, 1952–
   Coyote's council fire : contemporary shamans on race, gender, and community / Loren Cruden.
     p. cm.
   Includes bibliographical references and index.
   ISBN 0-89281-566-3
   1. Shamanism. 2. Spiritual life. I. Title
   BL 2370.S5C78   1995   95–32363
   299' .7–dc20   CIP

Printed and bound in the United States

10 9 8 7 6 5 4 3 2 1

This book was typeset in Bembo with Xavier Sans used as the display typeface

Destiny Books is a division of Inner Traditions International

Distributed to the book trade in Canada by Publishers Group West (PGW), Toronto, Ontario

Distributed to the health food trade in Canada by Alive Books, Toronto and Vancouver

Distributed to the book trade in the United Kingdom by Deep Books, London

Distributed to the book trade in Australia by Millennium Books, Newtown, N.S.W.

Distributed to the book trade in New Zealand by Tandem Press, Auckland

Distributed to the book trade in South Africa by Alternative Books, Randburg

Contents

Introduction

A great deal of soul searching has gone into the writing of this book. On the one hand, the experiences and thoughts presented here address issues at the heart of the shamanic community, issues in need of open discussion. On the other hand, these issues are volatile and emotionally loaded, and my perspectives and those of the shamans who speak in these pages may offend traditionalists and New Agers alike.

My intention, however, is not to air grievances, promote certain beliefs, or cast negativity in any direction. I write with an awareness of the perils of using personal experience as a basis for generalities. Yet because my experience, as described in the pages that follow, has extended beyond the conventions of my race and gender, there may be value in sharing these reflections. What seems important is not that I be persuasive but that we work to clear fear and illness of relationship from these precincts of race, gender, and community, allowing them to be places where we can look each other in the eyes without bitterness or shame.

No spiritual path has validity without love. No healing, whether of self or of world community, can be realized without compassion. The deeper our separations and disrespect, the deeper the wounds that bleed our power to move in a sacred way together.

I have omitted the names of many of the people I describe here because, although the stories are personal, the point of them is to name forces at work, not people temporarily embodying them. My own participation is not without regretful mistakes. I am profoundly grateful for the understanding, support, insight, teaching, and kindness that has characterized my encounters on the "Red Road." I give particular thanks to Lewis Sawaquat, Grey Wolf, Nina Wolf, Medicine Hawk, and Axis for gifts of friendship and collaboration at crucial times along this path.

With the increasing interchange between Native and non-Native spiritual seekers and teachers, there is a concurrent need for deeper understanding. This book explores some of the fundamental beliefs and arenas of contention that underlie and affect such interchanges. To reweave a web of kinship we cannot use threads that are unsound or that link us to suffering instead of well-being. Each thread must express awareness of spiritual priorities.

Beginning anew, we can still honor what has gone before and what joins us—but in the freedom that comes from our commitment to what each heart realizes to be sacred. With this commitment as reference, communication can serve healing.

The three parts of the book investigate race, gender, and community in relation to contemporary shamanism. In the essay that opens each part, I try to look beyond rhetoric in a process much like picking up a familiar object and turning it over and over in my hands. The interest is in seeing it anew and from all angles. This process doesn't reach for definitive answers or places for the mind to set itself down in secure conclusion. Instead, my intention is an examination informed by perceptive experience not unheedful of other voices.

Some of these voices are heard in the central portion of each part, where I pass the talking stick to other experienced teachers and healers so that this book can become a council of perspectives. These voices—male and female, Native, métis and non-Native—speak from diverse viewpoints around the wheel of truth. Rather than looking for opinions that mirror my own, I have sought voices that speak from long engagement in spiritual work. These are voices of experience and commitment and as such have my respect, if not always my agreement.

The old way of counciling together is one of giving quiet consideration to each speaker's words. There is no interruption, no timekeeping; each speaker is given respectful silence until he or she is finished. Rather than react to each other's words, councilors express what is in their own hearts and minds.

During the writing of this book I sent copies of a questionnaire to a group of teachers and medicine people, some well known, some not. Some are my personal friends, some I know only through correspondence or through their work. All have long experience with shamanic or land-based spiritual practices.

Some of their responses were general statements reflective of beliefs and spiritual alignments. Others more specifically addressed the questions I had posed. There are differences of opinion among various respondents, and also common threads weaving a web of shared engagement with truth.

What struck me most as letters arrived was the pervasive willingness of these spiritual veterans to reveal their hearts with eloquent simplicity. Instead of self-righteousness or smoke screens of spiritual platitudes, I found an ongoing inquiry into reality. None of these people were coasting on dogma or pat answers. A strong current of honesty and sincere examination flowed through these responses, touching and heartening me whether or not I agreed with the perspectives offered.

The area of most divergence was plainly that of gender issues. As a group, the women who answered the questionnaires were more traditional than the men. In its variety this council presents outspoken, strong-minded, and often emotionally charged positions without apology or fear—a model of speaking and listening across apparent boundaries of race, gender, and separate beliefs.

I send gratitude to all who participated in this long-distance council: exceedingly busy people who could have easily just tossed the questionnaires into wastebaskets and turned their attentions elsewhere.

I also thank Dr. Joan Townsend and Cat Saunders for their words and cooperation.

Each of the ten replies is quoted in full; in most instances a reply is divided among the three parts of the book, though a few are presented in one place in their entirety. I requested a biographical sketch of some sort, and a photo if possible, from each of the respondents, and those are as individualistic as the rest of the presentations. I made no attempt to regulate brevity or exposition, giving people free rein in how they wished to identify and express themselves. With those responses adhering to the questionnaire format, the questions are included also; where a question appears in one interview and not in another, its absence indicates that the respondent chose not to answer it.

Each part of the book ends with a set of contemplations, which may be useful for bridging points of view and for deepening understanding. These contemplations are for questioning and reviewing in a spirit of open-mindedness.

To use these contemplations, first relax and center yourself. Consciously release the clenched fist of tightly held opinions and put aside habitual patterns of response. Do your looking within from your dedication to live from the heart.

Be aware of what rises in your body, your emotions, and your thoughts as you ponder. Note what triggers a shutting down of calm inquiry, what makes you angry, disturbed, or sad. These reactions are signposts indicating places calling for deeper exploration. Acknowledge how you felt about things in the past. Kindly request that those guides rest while you muse on your own again as you may have done when you were younger. Let your adult surety take a backseat to your youthful investigator. Give yourself some freedom; don't mistake fixity for moral strength.

When your contemplation is finished I suggest leaving the door open for further insight or perhaps using the contemplations as springboards for discussions with others.

In the summer of 1981 the Michigan midwives' conference included a pipe ceremony conducted by a Potawatomie medicine man whose daughter one of the midwives helped deliver. The pipe ceremony took place outdoors. The medicine man's wife sat nearby in a rocking chair, baby at her breast, while her husband circulated the big pipe around the gathered ring of midwives. It was not a flashy ceremony. Beneath the quiet, good-humored manner of the medicine man was a depth of spiritual resource—a heritage and practice.

My own spirituality was influenced by an ever present but untutored psychic sensitivity. I didn't know how to respond usefully to all the many dimensions of reality that I perceived. My path was (and is) of the land. At the time, it was uninformed by esoteric teachings other than those attached to meditation. I relied on understandings derived from natural spiritual alignments and from my experiences with midwifery and herbal healing.

Something in the pipe ceremony resonated with my need, not for a teacher or a delineated path, but for clearer discernment of self in relation to the web of forces interweaving different levels of consciousness. Eventually I contacted the medicine man, Lewis Sawaquat, and asked if I could talk with him. He invited me to his home, about sixty miles from mine.

I was twenty-nine years old and had never told anyone the extent of my sensitivity. After hearing my description of some of the presences, precognitions, visitations, perceptive shifts, and other manifestations that I'd learned from childhood to keep silent about, the medicine man nodded and his wife said sympathetically, "There's nothing wrong with you, you're just psychic." When I heard those simple, accepting words, something that for all my life had been in a knot of fear—fear of madness and ostracism—let go. It was a pivotal moment of release.

The medicine man asked me, "Do you ever try to communicate with the spirit beings that you see?" I had not. It never occurred to me to see myself as a participant. That realization—which made me feel like a fool—was pivotal also. I asked the medicine man if he would help me develop a path where fear could be transformed and sacred use made of my skills. He agreed, asking that I bring him tobacco next time we met. There were two other requests Lewis made: that I keep a dream journal and let him read it, and that every morning and evening I go outside and pray in the cardinal directions.

Lewis Sawaquat was a dreamer. He had grizzly bear medicine and said that I should not be alarmed if he came to me in that form.

Looking at Lewis, no one could have trouble picturing him as a bear. The connection is evident.

The work with Lewis was not systematic. He would read my dream journal, then sit in a trancelike state giving me feedback on what he'd read. Some of what he passed to me was by direct spiritual transmission. Lewis's own medicine teachers had been Lakota and (I believe) Ottawa. Lewis's heritage is Potawatomie and Ottawa. His practices were derived not only from these ancestral ways but also from a European esotericism in which he was well versed. He would refer to such things as Western occultism and Celtic paganism, and he explained to me the rudiments of how to read Tarot. He was curious about all kinds of magic.

Perhaps this wide-ranging knowledge influenced his attitude about women. Perhaps it was just his Aquarian nature to be independent. At the time, though, I didn't realize how unusual he was. In his work with me Lewis didn't differentiate between men's and women's medicine ways or instruct me in traditional taboos. He urged me to talk to the spirits.

His relationship with the Native community at that time was strained by his associating with non-Native spiritual seekers, though he worked with only a few individuals and the teaching was private. It was some years before the tribe made full reconciliation by formally making Lewis the spiritual advisor to his people. In a recent letter to me Lewis stated with peaceful simplicity, "The tribe deals kindly with me."

Lewis Sawaquat referred to his path as the Red Road, yet he was not particularly interested in teaching me traditional or cultural formulas as much as he was in furthering an attunement to the essence of what underlies forms. Much of what I learned of ceremonial form came from observation and intuition, not instruction, and the understanding of essence came from practice and from a sharpening of awareness. The learning process was a dance of nuance, indication, and vibratory recognition, not of discursive lesson-receiving. Lewis opened doors and introduced possibilities. He shared his sacred ground, and this was a tremendous gift. I hadn't approached him to learn Native ways but to understand my own truth, and he was an ideal guide for this.

Some of the important aspects of spiritual work that Lewis demonstrated were:

- Freedom from imposition of sexual or racial prejudices
- Direct alignment with Spirit; connection with personal guidance and vision
- Humility and humor as medicine powers
- Equanimity in the face of ignorance
- Thoroughness in dealing with ceremonial forms and their implications
- Ongoing learning, curiosity, expansion, listening

A few months into the work, Lewis informed me that I was invited to attend a forthcoming sweat lodge ceremony. My attitude toward sweat lodge was that I'd never want to be in one. I had tried a sauna once and lasted five minutes before claustrophobia and discomfort drove me out. A sweat sounded a thousand times more difficult, and I had health problems to consider also. I tried to decline the offer. Lewis was uncharacteristically insistent. "You are *invited,*" he repeated, an ominous affability in his voice. I felt cornered.

"You don't understand, Lewis, I'll die in there! I'll at least pass out."

He smiled pleasantly. "If you pass out, you'll have people on either side holding you up—it's too crowded for you to fall over—and when you wake up you'll still be among friends and their good prayers." I gave up protesting but had trouble sleeping during the nights before the sweat.

The fire was lit at sundown. The ceremony's participants, including the two people sharing the fire tending, spent the hours between sundown and midnight in introspective preparation. Most of the people had attended sweats before, which was reassuring to the few first-timers.

By midnight the stones glowed brightly and the ceremony moved into the lodge. Lewis conducted it as a pipe sweat, and that aspect was deeply centering and strengthening. It was a lengthy, hot sweat, very powerful. The lodge was on the shore of a peninsula. When we emerged at dawn, four swans came winging at eye level along the beach only yards away from us as the sun rose over the still waters of Lake Michigan.

The two admonitions that Lewis gave me in that lodge have guided my work ever since. The first was that I must participate in life; and the second was that I must stay with my body when in the sweat lodge with others. The realizations that have flowed from those two simple directives have been profound.

Six years later, Lewis, who was diabetic, offered me tobacco in request for a healing sweat. It marked a shift in our association. I was startled into a laugh when he crawled out of that sweat and said with a groan and a smile, "You run a hot lodge, lady."

This was my introduction to Native spirituality. My own area of teaching and practice is that of native (of the land) medicine and not Native (of Indian culture) religion. Mine is a path indigenous to spiritual consciousness and experience of place and does not seek to imitate what belongs to tribal peoples. It is not core shamanism, neo-shamanism, or classical shamanism. It is simply a native spirituality.

Since 1985 I have done teaching and medicine work in my local communities, through correspondence, and in places far from where I live. If I had to give a name to this work I'd probably call it Natural Spirituality. It is the joining of life to Life. The pipe, the lodge, and the vision fast have, since my association with Lewis Sawaquat, continued to be sacred contexts I gratefully use and share. But this path unfolds in reference to constant realignment with the source, the Mystery that teaches, guides, and gifts me in each moment with the immediacy of life's sacred purpose. It is not the cloak of race or gender that determines this path; Spirit is the authority and Earth the nativity. In more than twenty years of living close to the land, with simplicity and gratitude, I have begun to touch an understanding of all my relations, and to share this in whatever ways serve a commitment to wholeness.

Because of Lewis's acceptance of me as a human being with certain capacities, I didn't think of the spiritual spectrum as having territories based on race, age, gender, or any other category. I didn't realize how wide the racial separations caused by pain and "otherness" had become through centuries of disrespect and persecution. My own words and actions toward Lewis and other Natives were not without blunders. Some of these were due to my lack of knowledge about Natives and spiritual protocols; some were due to a preoccupation with my own feelings and process. Understanding this, I still see interracial healing as possible. With a willing sharing there is no trespass. But first we must learn to ask and listen—to the land and to each other—not presume or demand, and to walk with mindful care together on sacred ground.

PART ONE

RACE

1

REFLECTIONS ON RACE

I remember sitting at my kitchen table with Lewis Sawaquat late one night, when everyone else was asleep. In the light of the kerosene lamps the medicine man's strong facial features were accentuated as he spoke with quiet intensity. On a paper he sketched a four-fingered flame and one by one named the fingers. "To know, to will, to dare, to keep silent . . . these are the directives of the old European magic."

He spoke about how to create a "body of light" with which to move in the spirit realms, and he said that the three necessary components of magical work were willpower, the ability to visualize, and emotional focus. It didn't occur to me to consider it odd that a full-blooded American Indian was teaching me about an esotericism belonging to my European heritage. It is one thing for Natives to speak about European spirituality and another for Europeans to present themselves as understanding things Native. It is like men talking about women. No matter what a man says, it'll sound wrong to women who are tired of having their lives defined by the dominant gender. Likewise, whatever Caucasians say about Natives sounds wrong to Natives who are fed up with being patronized or persecuted by outsiders.

Patronization and persecution of Natives are not just characteristic behaviors of the past. They are ongoing and deeply rooted. Until we reeducate ourselves about our relationships, problems of race will not be resolved. Oppression repeatedly finds expression through differences and misunderstanding. In contrast, maturity of relationship perceives differences without having them trigger value judgments or hierarchal separations. Racial interrelationships in today's world are still in a juvenile phase. The sense of self (whether racial or personal) is still based on the compare-and-contrast model, with our feeling of security dependent on some notion of superiority. Those with self-doubt or self-discomfort always look to competition for measures of worth. When whole races engage in this process, no territory is big enough to harmoniously encompass the adversaries.

Some years ago I was invited to an all-women's Sun Dance in the southwestern United States. The ceremony was organized by a group of lesbian Native women dissatisfied with the roles accorded women at Sun Dances on their home reservations. Unhappy with the discrimination they experienced as lesbians, they had come together to make their own Sun Dance.

In their letter to me they stated that non-Native women were welcome to attend as support people but only Native women would be allowed to dance. In my reply I suggested that prohibiting non-Natives from dancing seemed a perpetuation of the discrimination they were rebelling against. Personally I was not feeling pushed out. I was not planning to attend and didn't feel knowledgeable enough about Sun Dances to request such participation anyway. But it seemed incongruous that such a nontraditional Sun Dance should so mirror mainstream attitudes in terms of exclusion. At what point do disgruntled subgroups stop making their own categorical boundaries, which in turn create more excluded subgroups? Hierarchal division is inherently conducive to oppression.

I thought my letter more inquiry than censure but got an angry reply. After lambasting my attitude, the women said their elders would pray for me. (Fundamentalist Christians have told me the same thing.)

Someday perhaps the "exceptions" to racial generalizations will become so numerous that there will be no sense in dividing spiritual territory along the lines of race, particularly in our heterogeneous society. As this process unfolds and divisions lose their sharp edges, there are aspects of sharing that need consideration. The insistence of an automatic right to be part of whatever is attractive is, like hierarchy, an immature attitude typical of modern Western society. A careful path of inclusion seems wise when dealing with something as complex and cherished as spiritual heritage.

One of the drawbacks to this, however, is that decision makers may not always be seers with wide enough vision to ascertain what best serves the larger well-being. Decisions based on prejudice, convenience, vested interests, or constriction of discernment will neither preserve integrity nor invite positive change. Intelligent balance is not a sameness. Like the seasons it must follow a transformative movement that is alive, infused with power and natural duration. Like the seasons it must make sense in terms of long-range perspective.

It is certainly the right of tribal people to choose if and when to share their ceremonial occasions with others. But among these people there is no ongoing consensus. This lack of clear directive can be confusing to non-Natives, but it also serves to keep presumption at bay, bringing change more slowly. Already, ceremonies like the Sun Dance that once were tribe specific are becoming widespread and open to virtually all Natives choosing to attend them. Participation is gradually expanding as more and more exceptions are made that also include non-Natives or women.

Change always comes with sharing. In all evolutions something is lost and something gained. One of the losses from sharing ceremonial ways can be a quality of distinctiveness. Homogenization yields generic forms that no longer describe the view from a particular place of experience and insight. Homogeneous forms may serve unity, but will they also carry the power particular to spiritual relationship with place? Might unity reduce perspective? Usually it is tribal exclusivity that is seen as constricting and sharing that is thought of as expansive. In some instances this is true. But perhaps a more useful focus is on what basis the lines are being drawn. A path that shifts emphasis from racial difference to spiritual affinities could retain the distinction of its various ceremonial ways. If people can become spiritually oriented to the land instead of to race—in a bioregional, not territorial, sense—there could be not only interracial but also interspecies healing.

Ceremonial forms have always developed in conjunction with community and place. A bioregional spirituality rather than homogenization or rootless eclecticism might open relationships while preserving authentic diversity. Culturally and spiritually we are all borrowers anyway. The Navajo adopted many Hopi and Pueblo practices on arrival to the Southwest. Buddhism was influenced by the old Bon shamanism when it was brought to Tibet. Peyotism, exemplified by the Native American Church, moved into tribes to which it was not indigenous (as has the Sun Dance), and many religions and shamanic practitioners borrow freely from each other's teachings. Many Natives have incorporated both Christianity and New Age spirituality, as well as elements from other cultures, into their ceremonies and medicine ways. The notion of traditional purity is an illusion. Spirituality has never been a sterile environment. Orienting to the land makes sense in terms of survival as well as interrelationships.

The experience of sacred geography, which is a perceptive response to indigenous natural energies, both physical and spiritual, is something accessible to all. Certainly the specifics of how you abide with the land deeply affect perception and response. Few people, Native or otherwise, live in the old way. Even those who try are not untouched by modernity on some level, and the land itself is not as it was. But there continue to be modes of living and practices of awareness that open you to direct affiliation with the sacredness of Earth and Sky and their web of expression.

To live in healthy integration with habitat is to have access to its spiritual resources. Psychological distances between various races and cultures would diminish if the spiritual distance between people and habitat were closed. This does not mean a romantic reversion to the past; humans have yet to develop ideal ways of living harmoniously with each other and this Earth. Rather, it is a challenge to creativity, awareness, and vision. The return that needs to be made is not to some imagined primitive utopia but to a renewed priority of spiritual alignment. From that shift would emerge a collective yet diverse ceremonial expression, just as the many directions of the medicine wheel emanate from a shared center.

If all doors were to shut between the races, much could be protected of traditional ways. But in the long term such alienation would also foster more fear, stagnation, factionalism, and inability to communicate or cooperate. The world is no longer a place where our populations can insulate themselves in private corners of the planet. Sharing increasingly close confines, we become housemates on this Earth, housemates who need to realize some basis for sustainable cohabitation.

Modern-day Caucasians may protest that they are not accountable for racial atrocities of the past (or those of the present). Yet as members of the dominant North American race, we have a position that must be examined. I feel I can speak of this because as a woman—and a person living far below the poverty line—I have certainly experienced hardship, discrimination, and challenge to dignity and survival. I know how it feels to be a target of violence and disrespect based on gender or class. Despite this, as a European American, I can see a bottom-line difference in how I am regarded and in what I experience in society.

With the option of privilege is the concurrent responsibility to find ways to divest racial dominance of its controlling powers. It is not a matter of guilt. It is a real-life situation that can be changed as each of us addresses our part in it. The justice system, education system, government, lands, military, health care industry, media, arts, and religious establishment in the United States are controlled by European Americans. For the pyramid to become a circle where all voices are heard and universal well-being is attended to, there must be a willingness to let go of racial fear.

Part of the difficulty of this letting go is the concern that those who have lived without privilege will abuse the vulnerability of those whites who abandon the protection of racial dominance. This fear is not irrational. Good-hearted whites aligning themselves with Natives have been given demeaning labels by many Natives who accept their support. White women have been raped in some of these situations, and people painfully taken advantage of. It is naïve to think that hundreds of years of bitterness and disintegrating influences can be sweetened through wholesome intention alone.

The Native communities have agonizing challenges in the alcoholism, poverty, domestic violence, teen suicides, and related ills that have infiltrated their cultures in the wake of European invasion. But to say that their problems would be solved if whites just gave back the land and left—or to say that all problems began with the coming of whites—is to ignore both the irretrievable loss of their old way of life and the reality of what has since evolved.

Patriarchal religious and societal attitudes have been amplified in or have entered Native culture with the coming of Christianity to the West, touching all aspects of tribal community. Change must now arise on a primal level for both Natives and non-Natives. Interracial healing must be simultaneous with intraracial healing for all peoples. Heartfelt intention must be wedded to a development of spiritual capacity in order for cooperation to be more than superficial or fleeting. It is no longer just a matter of retribution.

The transgressions of whites have been discussed in the countercultural—and lately in some mainstream—media. Until there is a significant shift in the status quo, it is vital that this exposition expand and continue. But there is a disturbing side effect to the realization of how badly many whites have behaved to Natives (and lately to the Earth itself). That side effect for European Americans is racial self-hatred.

For over ten years there was an annual gathering in Canada initiated by a métis medicine man. His vision was to clear spiritual pollution from the world through sharing with non-Natives the wisdom of traditional medicine ways. Each summer Native, métis, and a few non-Native teachers and medicine people (mostly male) gathered at a site with a permanent medicine wheel set on it. Hundreds of non-Natives attended the encampment, which lasted several weeks, with a weekend at its center as the official event. There were sweat lodges, a large ring of tepees, and people tenting amid the trees. There were ceremonies, giveaways, and councils. Cree, northern Dine, Lakota, Kootenay, Colville, Arrow Lakes, Shuswap, Hopi, Apache, and other tribes were often represented. The non-Natives were mostly of European descent, though some were from Asian and African lineages. It was a complete medicine wheel of sorts, but something about it was off balance.

The first problem was that the medicine men often (and conspicuously) jostled for position. This was not an auspicious demonstration of wisdom, though it may have been the most ancient tradition enacted at these gatherings.

The second problem was that not only some Natives but also many whites could be heard fervently putting down the Caucasian race. The message being broadcasted was that whites are a bum race (or only fit for thinking up clever gadgets). I would wonder, when hearing some pejorative statement from a white: Don't you know what you're saying about yourself? About me? About your family, and your children, and your people? What does a racial self-image that is vile and monstrous do to one's ability to move in a consciousness of beauty? What is served in despising the face you see in the mirror or in denying who you are? Have we learned nothing from our assault on Native self-esteem?

There were Caucasians at these gatherings who knew land-based lifeways and who integrated those ways more deeply into daily living than had many of the Native teachers. There were non-Natives whose lives clearly reflected the spiritual vision that in some Native teachers seemed an aspect divorced from their behavior in other arenas. But the fixation on an idealized view of natives as the only keepers of wisdom built a wall around reconsideration of racial generalizations.

Each race, each culture, each person has teachings to offer—insights from their experience. One can learn as a step toward understanding without having one's own way threatened or without needing to imitate the ways of others. One can teach a path of sharing without claiming exclusive validity or becoming locked into changeless repetition. We can say to each other, "This is how it looks from where I stand right now," or, "This is the view of the cosmos my ancestors revealed to me, and it is part of how I see, too." Some of these views are cross-cultural; some are distinct to a people, place, or time. No race has a corner on wisdom or on folly. No race can walk through its history and not encounter violence perpetrated or received. Each race has ills to mend. Each race has spiritual knowledge to bring to the council fire.

The gathering was racially a no-win situation, though it was an important effort toward good relationship. No matter how sincerely the non-Natives abided by Native taboos and protocols, no matter how humbly and attentively they listened or how thoroughly they learned, they could never be Natives or be accepted as spiritual peers by most Natives. Instead they often ended up alienated from their own roots, their own intuitive relationship with Spirit, and their own racial dignity. For some of the Native teachers the exalted position they found themselves in left no room to deal with their own confusions and struggles, thus sometimes robbing their medicine work of integrity.

The gathering had two dimensions of experience. The first was the gathering of medicine people and organizers. For these people the gathering was often an emotional wringer fraught with logistical preoccupations, intense undercurrents, and unresolved interpersonal issues. It was also a place of prodigious dedication and love.

The second level was the event experienced by hundreds of seekers and celebrators who attended the councils, sweats, and ceremonies blissfully oblivious to the other dimensions. These people usually found the gathering to be a time of renewal or at least of uplift of spirit. How far these changes went into daily life is unknown, but that people derived a positive feeling, even a temporary one, seemed worth something. It was this paradox that kept the gathering in motion for more than a decade: the agony and the ecstasy.

We need to move beyond needy racial expectations to a mode of relationship that looks at competency, not skin color. At the same time—and for this not to be just another instance of European Americans being the only people with the circumstances to pursue competency—we need to attend to societal oppression of non-Caucasians.

For most modern whites, ceremony, whether primitive or civilized, is an intellectual and emotional experience. Modern European patterns of thought and belief overlay or at least interpenetrate spiritual experience. It is not often that this internal setting is dislodged or not basically present. The current European tendency to intellectualize or emotionalize spiritual experience, though it has its pitfalls, is not intrinsically better or worse than Native responses to Spirit. But it is unquestionably different.

It thus is important that interracial use of traditional ceremonial forms be done with care. It is too facile to call sweat lodges, drums, vision quests, rattles, and esoteric stone circles simply cross-cultural. Of course they are, but where, at least among Caucasians, are the unbroken strands of knowledge? What happens when the trappings of ceremony have no present reference point in community, habitat, or cosmology? Ceremonial form and paraphernalia have always existed within a matrix of beliefs, correspondences, and experiences. This relationship is usually detailed, extensive, and shared. Having a core implies that something surrounds or emanates from that center. The core without the apple is not much of a fruit.

This question will be returned to in part 3, reflecting on community. The aspect that I ponder here in relation to race is the exploration of nativity within ceremonial form.

There are several possible avenues to take when adopting ceremonial form. One is imitative. A form is used without understanding: because others are using it; because the idea of it attracts; because it is hoped that something good will come of using a proven form; or because it lends credibility to those using it. The drawbacks of imitation are obvious, though the dangers may not be.

Another possibility is to use an established form in a cross-cultural way, modifying it to be in accord with the cultural understanding and orientation of the user. Some ceremonial forms lend themselves to this more comfortably than others. Modification is objectionable to people who claim proprietary interest in the form. Others merely question whether the results of modification should carry the same name as the original. When does an outdoor introspection become a vision quest? What makes a person with a pipe a pipe carrier? What's the difference between shamanism and Jungian psychology? When is a sauna a sweat lodge? Names are full of important information and connotations to those who value clear communication or who use a shared semantics to carry significant understandings.

The more a specific form loses its distinct purposes and implications, the less meaningful it seems to be. With arbitrary modification the range of what may be included under a traditional naming is so wide as to empty the form of its particular attributes. Two people may speak of their "vision quests." One sat on a hill for a day to think about her life. The other rigorously prepared for a year, followed certain strictures, purified in a lodge, spent four days and nights in the wilderness fasting and praying, and ended with another sweat. Can both experiences carry the same name?

I'm not implying that the first person did wrongly or could not have had a profound experience. The discussion here is not of virtue but of clarity. Two people can refer to themselves as Pipe Carriers. One has been presented a nation pipe to use in a sacred way on behalf of a people with a continuity of relationship with the medicine pipe. The other person bought a pipe at a craft store and uses it to smoke pot at counterculture gatherings. Modifications may not always be changes that are useful evolutions of ceremonial form or naming.

Modification *within* tradition is of course more acceptable to those whose cultures have made long-term use of specific forms. Successive practitioners—and the times themselves—have always modified ceremonial forms to meet the needs of the people. Modification outside cultural continuity is a more complex matter. Here success is dependent on the modifier's depth of vision and resonance with the ceremonial form. When someone attunes to spiritual resource and guidance, changes in form can reflect a cross-cultural truth. This attunement usually includes an extended alliance with the land and the life patterns that are its language. It is not an intellectual process. It takes patience, stillness, receptivity, and skills with altered states of consciousness. What evolves from this in ceremonial form is then not without distinct purpose or connection to both local context and personal heritage.

When I hear Native songs in a sweat lodge, they seem to belong there. They feel linked to the essence of that ceremonial form. They resonate with the natural integration of lodge and land, seen and unseen forces, and the voices of the elements. This same feeling is in songs non-Natives have received during vision fasting or other deep communions with Spirit. But the songs and chants common to generic drumming circles, sweats, and ceremonies don't have that same resonance. They seem to express sentiment instead of experience. The words are nice, the tunes are sometimes appealing, but the power is not there.

This is not a racially imposed ineffectualness (maybe it is not ineffectual at all to those who are moved by these songs), but it is indicative of the different directions our cultures have pursued since the suppression of European shamanism. Caucasians seem to be struggling in a betweenness. Those trying to transplant traditions from their European roots find their severance from the past frustrating. Those engendering new paths are mostly cobbling piecemeal structures out of eclecticism, and those seeking an integration of their cultural roots with their current life situations are contending with Native reaction and the difficulties inherent to such an evolution. It is an awkward phase needing both more sympathy and more useful questioning than it's getting.

This betweenness, like all developmental stages, is full of opportunity for insight, dreaming, experimentation, and collaboration. It is a dynamic time, full of possibilities. We should not hastily seek niches that seem secure and defensible, but remember to be mindfully listening as well as courageous.

Joan B. Townsend, an anthropologist at the University of Manitoba, has written extensively on shamanism. In her paper "Shamanic Spirituality: Core Shamanism and Neo-shamanism in Contemporary Western Society" she writes:

> Core and Neo-shamanism, the two most prominent aspects of the [shamanic spirituality] movement, rose from similar bases, but they developed very different goals as well as approaches both to shamanism and to spirituality. Harner's Core-shamanism, discussed first, is a conservative, "purist" approach to traditional and contemporary shamanism. Neo-shamanism, on the other hand, uses idealized and metaphorical images of shamanism and attaches these to a wide range of rituals and beliefs not directly related to shamanism. Although one may find some overlap between the two, their foci remain distinct.
>
> Core shamanism, with Michael Harner as originator and prime mover, is a collage of universal elements of shamanism, particularly shamanic states of consciousness [SSC, a term Harner (1980) originated], and undertaking journeys into spirit reality to gain knowledge and heal. It attempts to extract what is fundamental to shamanism as it is found throughout the world without becoming entangled in specific cultural manifestations.
>
> Neo-shamanism is much more amorphous than Core-shamanism and its origins and leadership are diffuse. . . . It is a quintessential bricolage of parts of some shamanic traditions, reinterpretations of Harner's system, infusions of assorted rituals and beliefs from non-Western (often Native American Indian) spiritual traditions, and complete inventions, a few of which may

have come through traditional shamanic means of instruction by spirits during journeys.

While her perspectives are harsh in regard to neoshamanism and favorable toward core shamanism (with which she has personal experience), Townsend omits mention of shamans who are neither of those categories nor of the classical mold. These are the experiential, visionary shamans whose teachings come not from workshops and books (either Harner's or New Agers') or from cultural training but from direct engagement with Spirit. Regardless of what particular or eclectic practices they use in their work, these shamans focus on direct spiritual alignment, not on metaphoric beliefs or on techniques. The forms they use express rather than guide their alignments. This focus yields a practice similar to that of classical shamans in many ways, being affiliated to the source instead of the form of traditional medicine. In my experience these shamans tend to be solitary thinkers not much drawn to workshops, gatherings, or other people's ways of doing things. Their spirituality has a genuine—not idealized—connection to elemental forces and to the realms of mystery. In Native communities they may become medicine people (or heyokas). In non-Native society some of them are gaining recognition as healers and teachers.

In the urban setting it is difficult to sort through the plethora of workshops, practitioners, and groups to find who is doing what in the name of shamanism. Categories such as neo, core, traditional, and so on may help the sorting process and give food for thought. They may also encourage factionalism instead of providing a wider basis for discussion. There is more overlap between core and neoshamanism than would be supposed from Townsend's delineations. Core and neoshamanists both primarily use their paths for personal development rather than for mediation with the spirit worlds on behalf of the community. Practitioners of both tend to be middle class, urban, educated, and involved with various therapies or spiritual practices. Neither group has had much exposure to traditional shamanism or shamans. Both learn their basic techniques through workshops and books, and both tend toward eclecticism, though neoshamanists more explicitly so. Both groups also contain a wide range of practitioner effectiveness. As I said in a letter to Dr. Townsend, "I think [shamanic] experience depends more on a person's basic alignment of consciousness, the orientation of their intentions, and their beliefs about self than whether they are a core or a neoshamanistic practitioner."

Townsend fears that for New Agers, neoshamanism "may be a sterilized venture into their own minds," an adulteration of Native ritual marked by "crass commercialism and charlatans." Her concerns, I hope, will awaken people involved in contemporary shamanism to a larger sense of how their pursuits touch the world of shamanism as a whole. Her words urge a deeper and more thoughtful look at where these currents within the spirituality movement are leading.

Natives have their own dilemmas. As we bump into each other or circle warily over issues of ceremonial form, or who owns or can buy what, or who is a real medicine person and who is not, we can't forget that pain often masks itself as anger or hatred. The recognition of pain can make a useful difference in how we listen and respond.

One year I was gatekeeping at the Canadian gathering mentioned earlier. A car full of Natives pulled up, driven by a man my age. We talked for a few minutes, and as he prepared to enter the branching drive into the campgrounds I asked if he had been there before. He answered with glaring coldness that his people had been here for six thousand years.

His confrontational tone was disconcerting, and I could think of nothing to say except that the driveway might've changed in that time. I thought my reply might make him smile, but it didn't. Sometimes there is a starkness that will not allow approach except in its own time. It did trouble me that this man, who habitually courts Caucasian women, was so aggressive about race. It does no good to pile resentment on resentment, anger on anger, fear on fear. Acknowledgment of suffering is a step toward words and actions that serve healing rather than self-righteousness.

It seems unlikely that anyone connecting with land-based, natural spirituality in North America will not end up using ceremonial forms and accouterments that closely resemble what Natives have used. It seems inevitable given a common terrain, Natives' past examples, and human consciousness. Attempting to avoid all things Native-like as a way of avoiding conflict—or of honoring Native rights—may be to deny basic truths of human heritage and perception.

If the personal medicine way is a path one's own feet have walked, and on which one perhaps finds the moccasin prints of predecessors along the way, then ceremonial forms are manifestations of a shared nativity. The practitioner is then not a "wannabe" but is walking with a reference system that includes ancestry, place, connectedness, and ongoing awareness.

I could not say to a Native looking at my lodge, drum, feathers, medicine bundle, and so on, "This has nothing to do with Indian tribal ways," because obviously it does. Neither would it be true if the Native looked at these things and said to me, "This has nothing to do with you, white woman." My certainty of this rests on several aspects of experience. One of these is my repeated discovery of traditional techniques, uses of objects, or shamanic states (and accounts of experiences within those states) that were already familiar to me through personal practices and realizations. It is uncanny how closely I find these mirrored in my experience, though I arrived at them independently.

The second aspect that suggests that native spirituality is not race specific is the difference between people of the same race who live in different areas, which is often greater than that between people of different races who live in the same area, *if those people's levels of attunement to place are the same*. Alignment with natural rhythms, daily engagement with the elements, respectful awareness of spiritual and ecological webs, and a sensibly humble acknowledgment of humans' relative place in the larger cosmos, all characterize an indigenous attunement that is linked more to lifestyle and beliefs than to race.

The knowledge and medicine that are made accessible through that attunement do not discriminate between Native and non-Native, man and woman, elder and child. Instead, that medicine asks, "What is feared?" It questions patience, commitment, sensitivity, humor, sense of proportions, and love. It questions beliefs, dreams, and presumptions. It does not judge by skin color but, in the long run, may have a criterion more demanding (if less arbitrary) than that of race. It is the experience of these questions and demands that leads me to the reality of native spirituality.

The third aspect is effective practice. A connection to source is the foundation of vision, community integration, and continuing cycles of application and renewal that can produce transformative medicine work. This connection to source describes a practitioner's spirituality more accurately and usefully than does race.

The primary divergence in native and Native spirituality is cultural, not spiritual. Lineage, community, cosmology, beliefs, and tradition wove the threads of native attunement into the whole cloth of Native culture. This is a vital difference. The Native medicine person is at the heart of the tribe; the non-Native medicine person is at the fringes of society.

"Go honor your own spiritual roots and traditions," the non-Native is told, as if there were some womb to return to; as if there were no fences around Stonehenge; as if we are not all immigrants of one sort or another. There is a larger tradition than that of religion and tribalism, and that is of spiritual relationship with Earth and Sky. Modern people can weave new blankets from those ancient threads. They need not steal those of Native cultures, nor imitate their patterns, nor try to resurrect what has been buried. They need not wander naked at the edges of society, nor dress their truth in mainstream polyester. There is a sacred dream within modern people that can be awakened and embodied in harmony with all other paths of Spirit.

One of the causes of friction between Native traditionalists and the "rainbow" shamanistic movement is that many people adopting shamanistic practices have no sense of the ongoing reality of Native religion.

Believing you were Native in a past life, reading non-Native books purporting to be Native perspectives, watching movies that appear to portray Native experience, attending shamanistic workshops, or having Native-like paraphernalia does not accurately inform you of Native reality. Media images of Natives are almost categorically ridiculed by actual Indians. Their reviewers dismiss popular books and films whether they are current or from the days before Natives became "popular."

There are books written by Natives. There are Native Studies courses taught by Natives, and there are real, live Native people. All of these are better sources of information, insight, and experience than those offered by the money-conscious, truth-sacrificing media. This is not to imply that Natives aren't saying confusing or racially biased things about each other (or about non-Natives), but whatever their perspective may be, it is a Native perspective. Unfortunately, many people are not interested in Native reality. Today's Indian's life doesn't fit the required romantic image. People looking for escape from the fearfulness or tedium of the modern world are often more interested in a Celtic or Egyptian or Native American fantasy than truth.

Some people invest their beliefs in negative rather than romantic images of Natives. During a stay at the Canadian gathering I was sitting with one of the "dog soldiers" in my car, parked at the gate. It was after midnight and the camp was asleep. During previous gatherings some attendees had been harassed or even beaten up by locals. Most of the incidents had taken place at one of the nearby swimming holes. The area is economically depressed, reliant on resource extraction, tourism, and pot growing. There was always a simmering resentment toward Natives and outsiders (particularly urban outsiders) who arrived each year to occupy the old fairgrounds/sacred site where locals liked to party.

As we sat talking in my car that night, the quiet was shattered by a convoy of broken-mufflered pickup trucks bouncing and roaring through the tent-strewn camp. Headlights flashed over trees, tepee covers, and outraged, frightened faces peering from tent openings. The trucks blasted through camp—fortunately not flattening children in their sleeping bags or squashing lone souls walking to outhouses— and raced past us out the gate. (They'd snuck in through a sidetrack.)

I followed at the urging of the security person in my passenger seat. A quarter mile down the gravel lane the trucks suddenly stopped three abreast, blocking the road. An alarming number of tough young men (and a few tough young women) spilled out of the cabs brandishing tire irons and bats.

I stopped thirty feet behind the trucks, leaving my headlights on. My passenger got out and walked to where the mob waited. Heart pounding, stomach knotting, I began to pray. As the security man talked, the locals pressed around him, shouting, raising weapons, exuding drunken bitterness. I prayed aloud, gripping the steering wheel.

Behind me headlights approached and I heard gravel flung from running feet. A group of men from the gathering panted up to join the mob spotlighted by my car. A truck, leaving its lights on also, parked about fifty feet behind me. A Native medicine man stepped out and calmly stood beside his truck to observe the drama.

With the arrival of the men from camp the locals were stirred again to battle lust. I heard a woman's shrill voice urging, "Hit 'em! Hit 'em! What are you guys waiting for?" There was more yelling and raised clubs. Insults and challenges were hurled. Yet something held. Some restraint in the men from camp—a restraint that was not cowardice—caused a hesitation. Voices gradually lowered and calmed. In the lurid glow of my headlights I saw the tiny figure of a mouse sitting on its haunches on the roadside, watching.

Occasional angry shouts of "no-good Indians!" or "city faggots!" rose above the grumbles and growls as the locals began to talk to the men from camp. The medicine man's son, sundance scars on his chest, did not wince at the racist imprecations. The hippie bedecked in brocade and bells kept breathing and listening, and the martial artists stood relaxed and smiling as they eyed the tire irons clenched in frustrated fists. After a while it was over. Most everyone shook hands and the two groups parted company.

The next day some of these locals returned to the camp. This time they stopped at the gate and talked with me before (slowly) driving in to spend some hours checking out what the "Indians and faggots" were doing. The day after that they returned again, with horses to give children rides on. In following years there were no more incidents of violence between locals and gathering participants. The guys with the horses sometimes showed up, setting kids on the saddles in front of them as they carefully wound their way between tepees.

Images and the emotions they invoke can be dispelled and healed through real-life experience that offers mutual dignity. Healing begins with acceptance, the freedom from fear and intolerance. This freedom creates a space for all races to move in beauty. Acceptance is not the whole of healing, but it is its seed.

2

PASSING THE TALKING STICK

GREY WOLF

I was born in Vancouver, British Columbia, on February 12, 1924. Most of my first twelve years were spent in the Caribou region of south central B.C. The Native people who live there are of the Shuswap nation. I managed to get a grade school education. I was in the Canadian Army for a time. After that I got married and fathered four children. After they were educated I decided to try to relearn something of my Native heritage.

I made a circle of Turtle Island. North, east, south, west, and then north again. I visited many nations, always asking, "teach me what you wish." From this I took what felt comfortable to me and left the rest. My ideas came to be known as the New Nation due to the mixing of many teachings. Those of us who follow this path have become known as the Wolf Clan of the New Nation. We have no formal organization. I have become known as Grandfather Grey Wolf.

Once I was told by an Elder for whom I have great respect that all roads lead to the Center, it is just that some are a bit rougher than others. The one that I chose for myself has been quite easy going most of the time. Really very simple unless I choose to complicate it.

1. How do you see the relationship between race and spiritual orientation?

I do not find much connection between race and spiritual orientation, but I do find a lot of connection between culture and spirituality, especially where a culture has a strong religious connection. It seems that I connect religion to spirituality, or perhaps that some peoples have allowed their spirituality to become a religion.

2. Do you see a difference between Native (of Indian culture) religion and native (of the land) spirituality?

It is my feeling that religion dilutes or perhaps crystallizes spirituality. I try to follow the teachings of nature. I guess this could be referred to as "of the Earth."

3. Do you think that "core shamanism" can replace or be a useful adjunct to cultural shamanism?

I am not sure what is meant by "core shamanism." For that matter, I am not sure what "shamanism" is. I think of it as being in contact with the Oneness of All.

4. What are your feelings about non-Native use of traditional ceremonial forms? About modification or culturally based changes in those forms by non-Natives?

Which Natives? Which traditions? Are these copyrighted? Should I apply for a registered trademark? For myself, I feel honored if someone is comfortable with the way that I do something and uses that way.

5. Do you think the popularization (and commercialization) of shamanism has had a negative effect on Native communities?

I have been told that some people resent others doing some of the things that they believe they have an exclusive right to. I have been told that some believe that their young ones will not respect their ways if "everyone" is doing the ceremonies. I believe that things of the Spirit are gifts from the Creator and should not be charged for when passed on to others. I do accept honor gifts.

6. As a métis, have you experienced racial bias that obstructed (or attempted to obstruct) your spiritual work?

I have not experienced racial bias, but many times have been told that I was not doing things the Right Way. I have interpreted this as meaning that I was not doing things in the way that my critic would do them.

7. Do you feel that non-Natives should adopt traditional taboos as part of their involvement with shamanism?

I am very critical of taboos for myself. At this time I feel that I have freed myself of all that my culture—and others—have imposed on me in my past.

8. How do you feel about Native ceremonies being opened to attendance or participation by non-Natives?

My feeling is that it is entirely up to the individual who is conducting a ceremony who they invite to take part and how they want the participants to conduct themselves.

9. Do you think that ceremonial forms such as sweat lodge, vision quest, and shamanic drumming are cross-cultural, or are they particular only to Native cultures and their global correlates?

What some consider to be ceremonies may be daily routines for others. I do not feel that any culture has exclusive ownership of a way of contacting one's higher power or inner self.

10. Do you feel personally free of racial bias or anger?

I must confess that I do catch myself on the verge of adopting judgments of cultures and religions. I am not sure if this is residual cultural programming or just part of human nature. As soon as I become consciously aware of these thoughts I take measures to rid myself of them.

Nina Wolf

Galactically: One White Magnetic Dog
Cascadian: Nema Walking Wolf
US GOV: Nina J. Wolf
Birth Certificate: Nina J. Agins
Tribal: Benjamin
Blood: Ashkanazi, type A

I am an artist, teacher, celebrant, widow, parent, clown, storyteller, grand-
parent, poet, dancer, lover, and a fool.
I am a West Coast woman.
A habitant of Cascadia.
I live by the skill of my hands, the quick of my wit, the love of my heart
for you.
I have sixty-two summers.
I am supported by the villages and the friends of my heart and by the
beloved Earth, to whom my practice is dedicated. From the many stories
and images from the Old and New World villages that I carry, there are
a few that teach us how we may live in balance, in service, to the Earth
and each other.
These are my work.
These are my gift.
Teaching, counseling, healing, ceremony, ritual are all tools that help me
help others.

It is necessary for me to define *race* before I begin this section. This
will perhaps clarify my responses.

Race: classification of human beings by their shared physical characteristics; descendants of a common ancestor; distinct variety of human
species, a peculiar breed; lineage; descent.

1. How do you see the relationship between race and spiritual orientation?

True spirituality knows no race. Relationship to spirituality comes
through the family, the tribe/village, culture.

2. Do you see a difference between Native (of Indian culture) religion and
native (of the land) spirituality?

If by Native American religion the question refers to the specific
practices of a specific people living on a specific piece of land, then
I understand native land spirituality to mean the practice of people in
relationship to their living on and with the Earth. This, then, would
be an Earth-oriented spiritual practice determined by the place and its
interrelationship to the individual and the family. Such practice may
be arrived at through tradition, occupancy, intuition, sensitivity, observation. If the above is true, then "native spirituality" is available to
all people and not restricted to specific tribal affiliation.

3. Do you think that "core shamanism" can replace or be a useful adjunct to cultural shamanism?

What is "core shamanism"? Is it the contemporary practice of synthesizing tribal shamanic practices, averaging out the practices and states of consciousness, and then training people to perform the program? In ignorance, and off the top, I think core shamanism is dangerous to the individual and then potentially dangerous to the community. Unless shamans are deeply grounded in their place on the Earth, and within their community, their discrimination might be severely imbalanced. Cultural shamanism is a hermetic system. That is, it can only be learned as one is ready to accept and integrate each new teaching. Core shamanism seems to assume that all levels of experience are teachable at any time. I am writing without sufficient knowledge of core shamanism.

4. What are your feelings about non-Native use of traditional ceremonial forms? About modification or culturally based changes in those forms by non-Natives?

There exists in each tribe with a viable medicine tradition those whose job it is to preserve exactly the ceremonies and rituals of that tribe. There exists in each tribe with a viable medicine tradition those whose job it is to change traditional ceremony and ritual so that they will have meaning for each new generation. Tradition does not survive unless it is changed. My teachers are those visionaries who have seen that the Earth cannot be put back into balance by just the people of Native blood. These teachers selected those persons of other cultures who might best carry the essence of the native Earth-based spiritual practice to others in a sacred manner. Non-Native persons using Native ceremony must think most seriously about the effect of whatever form they are using. For a non-Native person to follow a practice of native, Earth-centered spirituality is not an easy task. It requires strict self-honesty, deep and continuous involvement in family, community, and constant renewal of dedication. The non-Native person does not, in mainstream North America, have the support, understanding, and belief of a community. Many Native communities do not offer this support to their elders/doctors. If a non-Native practitioner uses a Native-based ceremony/ritual and it is changed to have meaning for that circle, and the form is enhanced in a sacred manner and with respect, then it is for good.

> *The Sacred Is Respect Applied*
> *Respect Is the Sacred Applied*

I was led to learn North American ceremony and ritual in my search for how people connect to elements of the Earth on this continent, and how they express that connection. I am the firstborn of my family; the first born in this New World. I have spent a life sorting through all kinds of experience, knowledge, and practice to find the essential forms of how people may live in harmony with each other, all life forms, and the Earth in this place. It is a hope that some of what I know and have learned are of use to those who follow. I have a gut-based fear reaction to questions of practice and race. I am a Russian Jew. My children are the last of their families. There are no more. When discussions of geno-cide take place in council, I remind my friends that there are enough people to hold council. I am *very concerned* about utterances that con-nect purity of race with spiritual practice. My racial memory can only elicit the fear that my Native friends who are advocating purity of blood, unchanging tradition, and separatism will release the hounds of violence and prejudice, whose blood lust does not distinguish between the imagined enemy and the friend. This latest popular separatist move-ment may serve to elicit nationalism, tribalism, and increased powwow attendance. In a larger view, it can only serve to hasten the cultural genocide that the rhetoric says it wishes to prevent. So I'm going to place this issue in the center of the circle and let the winds blow. I'll walk the circle and listen. I'm waiting for the Grandmothers to speak.

5. Do you think the popularization (and commercialization) of shamanism has had a negative effect on Native communities?

Yes—as the public imagery is inaccurate, this has a negative effect. No—as positive public imagery is shared, this has a positive effect.

6. As a non-Native, have you experienced racial bias that obstructed (or attempted to obstruct) your spiritual work?

In British Columbia, where my work often included both Native and non-Native people familiar with native spirituality based on Earth centered practice, I encountered almost no racial bias in relationship to my work. (Please note I often had the assistance of male Native spiritual leaders.) In the U.S. there is great suspicion about my "credentials." Shamanism is based on a shared belief. A shared belief is an expendable commodity in a culture whose dominant feature is exploitative materialism.

7. Do you feel that non-Natives should adopt traditional taboos as part of their involvement with shamanism?

Yes, when these taboos enhance the power of the practitioner and are applicable outside of traditional use.

8. How do you feel about Native ceremonies being opened to attendance or participation by non-Natives?

Native, Earth-based spiritual practice is a hermetic system. The participant and the practitioner will only know/learn/perform what they are able at that moment to "know." The tradition is not fragile, nor does it need military protection. For example, Chinese folk art forms had "Western" content during the early transition to communism, but within ten years Chinese content had returned to Chinese folk art. Let the elders choose in their collective wisdom which ceremonies and rituals may be shared and which may not.

9. Do you think that ceremonial forms such as sweat lodge, vision quest, and shamanic drumming are cross-cultural, or are they particular only to Native cultures and their global correlates?

The drum, the rattle, the chant, the sweat lodge, the vision quest are part of every culture. To limit the use of these forms to protect the supposed vulnerability of the North American Native medicine tradition would not only be oppressive, it would be impossible to enforce.

(Questions 5–9 remind me of the early consciousness raising in the beginnings of the black, women's, gay, and lesbian rights movements. There seems to exist a pattern in contemporary North American social evolution/revolution for minority groups. These questions seem to fit into the pattern of growing self-awareness. The self-awareness is good. The isolation, misdirected anger, and violence do not seem to be social goods.)

10. Do you feel personally free of racial bias or anger?

Am I free of racial bias? Perhaps not 100 percent. I live in North America, so undoubtedly I am tainted by the cultural forms I live in. Conscious racial bias is not one of my major disabilities. Am I angry? No. Sad sometimes, defensive . . . sometimes. Not angry. I do not carry the White Man's Burden. I am not blinded by sentimentality or by romantic notions. I know the results of misplaced anger.

LEWIS SAWAQUAT

Lewis is the spiritual advisor to the Grand Traverse Band of Natives in Michigan. He is a medicine man of Potawatomie and Ottawa ancestry, an elder and spiritual leader of his people.

1. How do you see the relationship between race and spiritual orientation?

It probably neither helps nor hinders. I suspect, however, that it influences the direction one follows toward the light.

2. Do you see a difference between Native (of Indian culture) religion and native (of the land) spirituality?

The same. However, if there are variations, how much may be due to contemporary influences?

3. Do you think that "core shamanism" can replace or be a useful adjunct to cultural shamanism?

Sure.

4. What are your feelings about non-Native use of traditional ceremonial forms? About modification or culturally based changes in those forms by non-Natives?

There are many different kinds of shamanism, each with a rich and beautiful interpretation of the primordial truth. Let us learn from one another in a nonexclusionary way.

5. Do you think the popularization (and commercialization) of shamanism has had a negative effect on Native communities?

Yes, of course, in a powerful manner. But it has on other sincere practitioners also.

7. Do you feel that non-Natives should adopt traditional taboos as part of their involvement with shamanism?

If well founded in truth, a truth that can be enunciated in words, then yes.

8. How do you feel about Native ceremonies being opened to attendance or participation by non-Natives?

The red path is the path of life; all life, all species, all sexes, all colors, etc. No life form is excluded.

9. Do you think that ceremonial forms such as sweat lodge, vision quest, and shamanic drumming are cross-cultural, or are they particular only to Native cultures and their global correlates?

There is *one* initiator, the "divine" self or spirit. All life finds its beginnings (initiation) there. This truth has always been known by natural people. Any and all barriers that have since been imposed are artificial.

CHARLA HAWKWIND-HERMANN

From the Wind River Reservation in Wyoming to the network media boardrooms of San Francisco and Atlanta, I combine a unique background into the creation of Hawkwind Earth Renewal Cooperative, a spiritual healing center in the north Alabama mountains. As a writer and video film producer, I have worked on a documentary about Operation Desert Storm for CNN, the ten-hour video series Quest of the Earth Keepers, *and a new* Wisdom Women *series. The ability to tell the story of environmental crisis and healing has been brought into my work as an Earth teacher and ceremonial leader. I have dedicated my life to communicating a healing message that is functional while living in the city or in a tepee on a mountaintop. Living at Hawkwind with no running water for the past seven years provides a humorous balance to my fast-paced media career of twenty-five years. I have learned to walk my talk and live in harmony with all creatures, and I love sharing the joys of Spiritual Ecology with children and adults all around the country.*

1. How do you see the relationship between race and spiritual orientation?

Tarwater and I are both mixed blood with German, Scottish, and Irish in the family, and we both had families who were anxious for us to grow up as middle-class white Anglo-Saxon Christian, etc.

2. Do you see a difference between Native (of Indian culture) religion and native (of the land) spirituality?

Yes and no. Yes it makes a difference as to what you are exposed to as a child. The orientation of your parents' spirituality most definitely jades the perspective of a child. I have seen whites as adults become very comfortable with many spiritual dogmas—Yoruba, Huichol, Native American, African, and Buddhist, to name a few. I have noted, however, that very few African, Mexican American, or Asian people have felt comfortable in doing hard-core ritual on the reservations of this country. You see every race involved in Christianity, and the reverse is more prevalent than most would suspect. I took world religion courses for years and always found that people from every race were curious and needed to connect with what was "higher" and more meaningful to their own hearts. As I grew up on the Wind River Reservation and became a longtime Sun Dancer with the Lakota and Arapahoe, I found that the average Native American has more Christianity in all practices than a "Rainbow" who practices Native American ceremonies. For instance, only 20 percent of the Lakotas on the Rez go to sweat lodge or vision quest, and only 2 percent sundance, though over 50 percent honor the dance and the pipe as sacred. Only 5 percent ever learn the ceremonial language and attempt to lead ceremony for any other than their own family. The Rainbows have a much higher percentage of those who get involved and those who become serious ceremonials. There are far more Rainbows sundancing right now than full-bloods. This is happening worldwide.

3. Do you think that "core shamanism" can replace or be a useful adjunct to cultural shamanism?

I do not know what you mean by core shamanism. I do not know anyone who practices Medicine on the Rez who calls themselves a shaman and none have a pink business card to tell people where to find them. They just "are," and their magic is nurtured through years of strong spiritual adherence. I don't think that most whites know what shamanism in its total state of altered consciousness is really all about. The best "shamans" or medicine men *(pejutos)* that I know could meet the low standards of any mental ward in the country. The great practicing healers of our time, like Brooke Medicine Eagle and Phil Lane, are not presuming to hang titles on their works. I am many things; a practicing healer has come out of spending so many years at the practice of healing my own wounds. The "tricks" of the trade will never be captured in a book or the label shaman.

4. What are your feelings about non-Native use of traditional ceremonial forms? About modification or culturally based changes in those forms by non-Natives?

I can do thirty-five lodges in a week at Pine Ridge with the top "medicine and holy" men and women, and have experienced forty versions of the lodge and styles of songs and pouring. I know fifteen versions of a single pipe song, each sung by a "real" Indian. These ways come to life when the intent of the ceremonialist is clear and the tools are used in a learned and respectful manner. The pipe was left to "the people"; Calf Pipe Woman did not say only one color or one heart, but that all hearts would be protected by these ways. Everyone has an opinion and a belly button. The right way to practice these ways is what works for the individual leader. I have provided ceremony for over twenty years, and no two ceremonies were ever the same, because the intent and the need were different. My understanding of the dogma changed when I let go of trying to find the right rules. Any person of any race can get hurt playing with these ways. There is much ugly stuff done in the name of greed and power, and these are delicate balances that get tipped far too often in every religion.

5. Do you think the popularization (and commercialization) of shamanism has had a negative effect on Native communities?

Yes and no. Yes, many of my elders would cry if they knew how many women have been spiritually raped by sham-men. Yes, my elders would be offended at the outrageous ways that some people have dressed up to play wannabe. *But,* they are very pleased when any person of any race participates in a respectful way and receives a good healing. It is not appropriate for someone to be a corporate giant raping the land Monday through Friday and expect absolution by going to a lodge on Saturday night. That holds true for confessionals and sacraments of all religions. Meanwhile, the craft workers and teachers on the Rez *have* benefited from the popularity. The economy and travel to sacred places have increased revenues of many nonbelieving Indians. It has also trampled many a sacred site as pieces are taken from altars and pictures are taken of private matters. Native Americans are getting better media and less of a voodoo rap on TV right now and that is good. However, many is the time that I feel like I got invited to a party as a token Indian to show off. A long road traveled from the days when whites spit on us and called us "half-breed prairie niggers"!

6. As a métis, have you experienced racial bias that obstructed (or attempted to obstruct) your spiritual work?

I have found that being a part-blood or Rainbow on the Rez means that you have to do everything much better—fast longer, pray harder, dance harder, etc.—because so many "pink lighters" have made it seem airy-fairy and do not realize the solid/grounded nature of these ways. This is a hard path, and pink light goes fast. The weak at heart are weeded out really fast unless they have money and are financing some "medicine" family who keeps them around as a token white . . . funny world of balance, isn't it?

7. Do you feel that non-Natives should adopt traditional taboos as part of their involvement with shamanism?

I do not feel that flesh offerings or piercing have the same meaning to whites and are not honored in the old way as a healing tool, but are used more as a merit badge. I see many whites think, first you get the lodge badge, then the pipe badge, the drum badge, the vision quest badge, the dance badge, and then you must be a real shaman. It does not work that way. I have been like this all of my life; I worked with these same tools but found wiser and more mature expression of them throughout time. I was not afraid to die to live, but the dying was hard and painful. I was more scared than I ever knew I could be. A "wannabe" won't dance with death. They run to the next easy answer, and that's OK, 'cause that's how Spirit weeds out those who should not practice these ways.

8. How do you feel about Native ceremonies being opened to attendance or participation by non-Natives?

I have practiced these ways with every race, color, and size of person, as have my full-blood elders. I have always been taught that this is for the person who comes in a good way.

9. Do you think that ceremonial forms such as sweat lodge, vision quest, and shamanic drumming are cross-cultural, or are they particular only to Native cultures and their global correlates?

Native Americans are by no means the only nation with these practices. I have found extremely similar rituals all around the world. The drum is everywhere, and no one can or should legislate when, where, or how we pray.

10. Do you feel personally free of racial bias or anger?

No, I have many biases about being a mixed-blood. I spent over forty years getting comfortable with expressing my own heart over race. In my own family I had adopted brothers that were very dark, and Vietnamese sisters. I have seen and heard horrible things coming from the mouth of a white redneck in many languages. I always feel that I must really watch myself in rituals with my darker kin, as well. Though I am probably fairly "politically correct," my true heart knows that anger about ignorance and apathy of any race is still prejudice.

ED "EAGLE MAN" McGAA

Ed is a registered tribal member of the Oglala Sioux, born on the reservation. He joined the Marine Corps after earning an undergraduate degree and later received a law degree from the University of South Dakota. A fighter pilot and sundancer, he is the author of Red Cloud,

Mother Earth Spirituality, Rainbow Tribe, *and* Native Wisdom, *his most recent book. He currently resides in St. Paul, Minnesota.*

When relating to mystery, it is my supposition that none of us have total answers. Total answers cause wars and too much disagreement, which I do not want to be part of. "I could be wrong, totally wrong, and you might be right" is part of my philosophy and is stated strongly in this work. I also let it be known that I am influenced by the Natural Way, my teachers, my ongoing experiences, and other authors. I do not speak for any tribe. No one does.

From *Native Wisdom: Perceptions of the Natural Way*:

> There are some who want to keep the Natural Way to themselves, but among the very powerful holy men and holy women I have known, they believed that it should be shared.
> . . . Black Elk told his vision to John Neihardt to record and pass on. Ten years later Black Elk told the same vision to J. Epes Brown. It is quite obvious Black Elk intended this vision to be shared. My two main mentors, Chief Fools Crow and Chief Eagle Feather, also shared. Their truth was substantiated by their conduct. A very powerful indicator to me of their truth was their exceptional power and connection into spirit-calling ceremony. If a detractor states otherwise, I would want to know if he has equivalent power and substance in relationship to these three stalwarts, who believed that the only way for the dominant society to truly change was to learn from indigenous philosophy. If the dominant society does not change, we lose the planet. It is as simple as that.

The following is an article that I wrote in regard to conflict and the return of the Natural Way.

> In the 1960s we who were trying to bring back the Sun Dance had our hands full with the local Pine Ridge Reservation missionaries and, most critical, with our own Lakota people. The "traditionals" in those days were vastly outnumbered by the nontraditional Christian-espousing Indians, and they made it difficult for our great holy men, Chief Fools Crow and the Rosebud holy man Bill Eagle Feather. Now, several decades later, there are very few who will admit honestly that they opposed us. Just about everyone claims that they were all avid defenders of the Natural Way Spirituality.

Over a quarter of a century ago, I traveled with a real holy man, Bill Eagle Feather, a Sichangu Sioux. Once he found six bodies under the snow and ice from seven predictions made in his Yuwipi ceremony. I also learned from Chief Fools Crow, who was equally in tune with the spirit world. Both men were teachers and shared their knowledge. I also knew Ben Black Elk, the son and interpreter for the great Sioux prophet Black Elk. All three of these men named me Eagle Man just before we began a Sun Dance that the reservation missionaries were trying to stop. Ben had me carry his father's pipe in that Sun Dance.

There are many now who deeply respect native wisdom and its related prophecies. Some refer to these people as New Agers. Actually they are Old Agers because, unlike organized religion, these people respect Old Age philosophy and spirituality. Let us look at the world today. Who is bombing, shooting, torturing, and killing humanity? Who killed the thousands of Jews in the Holocaust? Who took the Indian lands and pointblank forbade Indian ceremony? Who put up the boarding schools? It is not the New Agers.

What church went hand in hand with the Spanish Inquisition and burned the great libraries of knowledge preserved for centuries by the Inca, the Mayans, and the Aztecs? Who calls Native American ceremonies pagan and heathenish and downgrades them as instruments of their own self-created devil? Why have so many older Native Americans been afraid to attend sweat lodge, spirit calling, Sun Dance, and other traditional ceremonies that did not beseech to the white man's God? Who brainwashed them to ridicule our beautiful ceremonies that beseech to a Great Mystery? It is not the New Agers.

In Bosnia, we saw three religions killing, raping, and fighting. Each believes that they have the sure ticket to God, and they don't bat an eye to kill over it. New Agers do not have this philosophy nor this track record to destroy our ways.

Like my mentors, I had hoped most Native Americans who knew their culture would see the need to educate the white man, and this would have been a challenging opportunity for Native and Indigenous teachers to go out and change the dominant ones for the better. There have been a few brave ones who have taught the white man, but not enough. This has been a great disappointment. But then again, Black Elk never lived to see the sacred tree begin to bloom, as I believe it is now.

Long ago, the recorded speeches of native American leaders all called on the dominant society to change. Our leaders were shocked with the disrespect of nature exhibited by the advancing immigrants. In all the speeches of the old Indian chiefs that I have read, every one of our leaders wanted the white man to change his ways, and many warned of serious consequences if this did not happen. When we enter the spirit world, the old chiefs will no doubt ask, and I would not want to be one of those that they will chastise eternally, "Why did you try to prevent the changing of the white man? Why didn't you teach the white man the Earth stewardship ways, especially when Mother Earth was in great danger?" Did we detract, squabble, and negate what was a sincere attempt to learn?

Many people in the dominant society have seen through the fallacy of organized religion and its weak values, and now they understand the Blue Man prophecy of Black Elk's vision—the Blue Man of Greed, jealousy, hate, and lies; the Blue Man who began by killing off the buffalo and issuing smallpox blankets and putting everyone in boarding schools in collusion with organized religion. This Blue Man certainly does not want Native Americans to share proven knowledge that will change the dominant society away from its present infatuation of Blue Man values that is infesting the Earth and poisoning with hate, crime, jealousy, and deception. All sacred sites will be eventually closed and the broken treaties will never be amended if the Blue Man wins. The Earth situation will get so bad that Indigenous people will have to go forth and educate, otherwise Mother Earth herself will bring forth destruction. Most, if not all, could perish. Great change upon the planet has happened before, and Mother Earth does duplicate and replicate. Down through time she has done so. Modern society is not immune to severe natural change. So be it. I rarely make a prediction, but this is my prediction.

I believe that Black Elk's vision is a true vision and that the Six Powers of the Universe declared that all two-legged should learn to live in harmony. Black Elk conveyed his vision in order for it to be learned. Why else did he tell his vision? I imagine that he will have much to say to his detractors when they enter the spirit world, for it is an extremely powerful vision and should not be thwarted. I also believe that the Natural Way is such a powerful force that it will sweep the world in its own due time. No one group of people or organization will be able to contain it. Ignorance, jealousy, and untruth will be employed by the Blue Man forces, however. If we do not all return to the Natural Way values, we will lose the planet and two-legged will be but a memory.

Some important issues regarding religious conflict are conduct within certain ceremonies, the use of the peace pipe, and sacred sites. The majority in this nation know little about the Natural Way. There are many who are doing more than just observing, however. There are those who seek to participate in natural beseechment or ceremony. To those people I suggest that maybe you should stay away from specific Indian ceremony if it offends others, but that does not mean that you should stop seeking Earth knowledge. If you are invited by Native people to ceremony, then respect their customs, their taboos. Be quiet. Be modest. Go slow. Do not be in a hurry. Do not aggrandize or exaggerate your experiences. These are important advisories. The most important advisory, in my opinion, is "Never stop seeking and learning." The Earth might be lost if you do. No one can take away your religious freedom, at least not unless the far religious right gets back into power. And do not think that they are not trying. They stacked the Supreme Court, and when that fails their next move is into the school boards and Congress.

In regard to a peace pipe, what do you need a pipe for to beseech? I use my wotai stone more and more because I am so disgusted with the argument involving innocent people who are not of Native American blood, wanting to beseech with a peace pipe. Who can keep you from picking up or finding your own special stone that is out there in Mother Earth? There are plenty of them. Pick up your stone that has been waiting for you down through time and lift it toward a direction and identify that which is good with that direction. Beseech to your higher powers in this manner and there will be less occasion for argument.

If you want to pray to your higher power, then go to an isolated place. Why go to where Native peoples are finding their areas becoming crowded? The four directions are everywhere; the Great Mystery, the Creator, is everywhere. The spirit world listens to all who are truthful regardless of where you are at. You do not have to be on Bear Butte, on Mt. Sinai, in Mecca, or at the Wailing Wall. To go up on a mountaintop or on a butte or into a lodge and beseech one's higher power—this is not a specific rite that falls under a jurisdiction of any special race, organization, or tribe. The Jews were doing this ceremony, vision quest, long before the Christians. The Celts beseeched to a Creator in lodges long ago. Across Europe and into Mongolia, spiritual saunas were held to beseech. No one owns beseechment.

All in all, religious conflicts are usually based on zealous precepts, arguments, dictates, holdings, proclamations, etc., and all brought forth by humans. I doubt if a single spirit has brought one issue forth. Common sense is my suggestion, and I certainly would not want to discourage anyone from seeking knowledge, wisdom, and understanding from the Natural Way or the Native Wisdom. I would thoroughly check out the background of anyone that does not want you to know more of the Creator's creation. What is their past? How were they to their children? How have they raised all their children, or do they have some offspring that they never supported? How did they treat their spouses or past spouses? Where were they when there were but few who stood up for the Natural Way? Have they always had a history of condemning and negativity? Are they optimistic about any issues? Are they seeking attention? What is their concern or knowledge regarding the environmental or planetary situation? Are they willing to introspect? These are important questions to ask.

Incidentally, I am not a medicine man and have never claimed to be one, nor do I intend to be one. I am an author, which I prefer to be. For myself, I do not think you have to be a medicine man to attempt to beseech or greet the spirit world.

I do not believe in charging for a ceremony and never have, because the Creator and the spirit world have provided for me in other ways. I also have turned down some lucrative opportunities to do what I am doing now. I could have been an airline pilot or a retired military officer with high rank, and I sure as hell do not practice law with my law degree, because the whole legal system is one of untruth and I do not want to be part of that. I have lost jobs because I was too honest. As an author, at least so far, I am allowed to be honest.

In regard to poor medicine people out on the reservations, I believe that people of means should financially help those who do not even have the means to travel. Too often we see or hear about some well-heeled Indian, professor, bureaucrat, or newspaper editor shooting his mouth off about these poor Indians who are walking their talk and have had to accept some financial help simply to eat. Donate and give to the poor medicine person and healer. Don't screw up this statement from me, however. Too many of those well-feds are trying to make rules in this area. My mentors were poor as hell, and I helped them out when I had the means.

Regarding the role of women, I am quite matriarchal. The absence of women having any power or leadership in organized religions is the main reason for their weakness. Too many of our tribes have been under the influence of organized religion for two to three centuries and have picked up their patriarchy.

BROOKE MEDICINE EAGLE

I am an American native Earthkeeper, teacher, healer, songwriter, ceremonial leader, sacred ecologist, and author of Buffalo Woman Comes Singing, *whose dedication is bringing forward the ancient truths concerning how to live a fully human life in harmony with All Our Relations. At home in the beautiful Flathead Valley of Montana, I am the creator of EagleSong, a series of spiritually oriented camps; and the founder of the FlowerSong Project, which promotes a sustainable, ecologically sound beauty path upon Mother Earth. I have studied with master teachers of many healing techniques, including medicine people of the Americas. I am a licensed counselor, practitioner of Neuro-Linguistic Programming, certified Feldenkrais practitioner, and high-challenge ropes course facilitator. Although an enrolled member of the Crow Indian tribe in Montana, I teach from my primary identification as a global family Earthkeeper—a sacred ecologist dedicated to nurturing and renewing the circle of life through the growth and healing of our two-legged family upon Mother Earth.*

1. How do you see the relationship between race and spiritual orientation?

The relationship seems to me to be a reflection from the past of the fact that certain religious practices were developed in various, relatively isolated parts of the world. *The basic truths of spirit are the same essential truths, from whatever perspective one sees them.* However, they are cloaked in different forms and accompanying rituals to fit the culture and land where they are practiced. A simple instance would be something like using sandalwood incense in India and sage in

North America. More complex differences result from the social/ spiritual development and emotional tone of the people. Today, races are mixed among each other and spread across the globe, as well as in their own old territory. Thus it makes sense to me that some of these people would change spiritual orientation. Also, given a global choice of alternative, rather than only the one born into, people have greater opportunity for experimentation, and for perhaps finding a way that seems to "fit" them better than what others of their race originally practiced.

2. Do you see a difference between Native (of Indian culture) religion and native (of the land) spirituality?

Each tribe or group has its own form of religion, its own practices, its own personal ceremonies that have developed over time. These certainly include an aspect of connection with the land. This native spirituality is the right and, I would say, the responsibility of *all* people; but I do not believe it is an outsider's right to practice specific rituals and ceremonies that belong to a certain tribe. For instance, purification lodges consisting of a small, enclosed space, hot stones, and prayer are generically human—this form of hydrotherapy has been practiced by people all over the globe. Thus, it is anyone's right to create a purification ceremony for themselves using these elements. However, to try to imitate, recreate, or use for example a "west door, doctoring, stone people lodge of the Lakotas" without full training and permission from the elders is absolutely not OK.

3. Do you think that "core shamanism" can replace or be a useful adjunct to cultural shamanism?

By core shamanism I assume you mean a generic shamanism, such has been practiced throughout the world and is viable and useful in all cultures today. Yes, I would hope that more and more people begin to view and act in the world through shamanic eyes—those that understand and interact with the spiritual realm in healing ways. Shamanic work seems not only to connect people who practice it to the world of Spirit but also, in a fuller and more healthful way, connect them to the Mother Earth and all her children—a movement vital to our survival at this point in history.

4. What are your feelings about non-Native use of traditional ceremonial forms? About modification or culturally based changes in those forms by non-Natives?

See #2 above. My statement above does not in any way seek to limit those who do not originally belong to a tribal or cultural Native group from seeking to learn those ways. In modern times I have seen as many young whites vitally interested in carrying on the traditional Native ways as I have young Natives. Many times the young Native people are seeking to become more mainstream, while young whites are awakening from the thrall of that mainstream way of life to seek something more whole and holy. I know quite a few holders of traditional bundles and ceremonies who are not members of the original cultural group, and I know that they have paid their dues with study, good relationship, and willingness to serve Spirit. They have been given these responsibilities by those with whom they apprenticed over long periods. Concerning modifications, I think it is important for people to look back as much as they can to the ancient forms of their own racial people, and they will often find that there was an Earth-based spirituality there which can serve them as a model. Yet our modern culture is different from anything in the past, and I believe that the Great Spirit understands the naturalness of change, as well as the deathlike quality of rigidity and refusal to change. Thus it makes good sense to me that modification in form, as people and cultures change, is not only necessary but essential. The challenge in the changes is to keep the eternal truths and change only the outward forms as appropriate.

5. Do you think the popularization (and commercialization) of shamanism has had a negative effect on Native communities?

Yes and no! First, no. Native spiritual ways becoming more popular has helped many people to realize the importance of preserving Native cultures, and among my students these ways have encouraged a vibrant spiritual ecology that advocates the support of Native peoples. However, there are Native people still in the victim/anger mode who would rather see the whole human race wiped off Mother Earth before they would want one of their conquerors' offspring to practice their ways. I don't find this a spiritual way of thinking, nor a useful one. When many Native people are pledged through the sacred pipe and other rites to All Our Relations, it seems to me they need to realize that all people (races) are thus included. And even just for the sake of their own children, having more and more people practice earth ways is important.

Now, yes. In a way, the commercialization of shamanism has a negative effect on everyone. I sometimes wonder if the practice of it will eventually bring those practitioners to a deeper, noncommercial approach, which is very basic to shamanism; certainly, preventing people from practicing those ways does not seem to be the answer. And given the nature of our media world, it seems impossible to enforce any guidelines Native or other people might set. In the old way, it is often said, "Give them to Spirit, who will give them their just reward." Of course, that was easier when the limited size of the tribal groups allowed much easier control of the practices.

6. As a métis, have you experienced racial bias that obstructed (or attempted to obstruct) your spiritual work?

As a métis member of a Native American tribe, I have experienced the reverse prejudice of reactionary Native people who feel I do damage by working with whoever seeks my services—mostly whites. This occurs even though I do not teach "traditional" ways, and although most of those who protest do not know me or my work personally.

7. Do you feel that non-Natives should adopt traditional taboos as part of their involvement with shamanism?

I can't make a general answer to this. Basically, one needs to go back to the *why* of the taboo to understand the reason for it. (This sometimes angers "traditional" people because they have long forgotten the reason for it and are simply following a form.) Once the basic sense of it is ascertained, it can then be applied to the present situation, with help from Spirit through prayer and meditation.

8. How do you feel about Native ceremonies being opened to attendance or participation by non-Natives?

I think it is entirely up to the Native people in each specific instance. I am ashamed of how some non-Natives act at ceremonies, though, and I think it would be good to put non-Natives through a little education of some kind before they are allowed in. This would be a good chance for Native people to interact in a teaching way with those interested in their ways, as well as a vital teaching in respect and intercultural consciousness for the non-Natives.

9. Do you think that ceremonial forms such as sweat lodge, vision quest, and shamanic drumming are cross-cultural, or are they particular only to Native cultures and their global correlates?

The specific forms you mention are obviously cross-cultural. For example, Scandinavian people do a purification/sweat lodge in their saunas, which is very clearly a spiritual practice (they simply use a wooden, stationary form because it fits their land and experience). Jesus fasted in the wilderness for forty days seeking guidance and vision—a classic vision quest. Etc., etc.

10. Do you feel personally free of racial bias or anger?

I wish I could say yes, because I work very hard at being free of it given the fact that as a métis I have been subject to it. I can only say that I feel the amount I carry is small and getting smaller.

AXIS

I am a male of the race of human beings, of mixed ancestry and pigmentation, depending on the amount of sun I get. I believe in not-believing (which is different from disbelief). My practice is of magick and focuses toward healing and awakening. I live and work on a farm in Wisconsin and practice martial arts incorrectly.

1. How do you see the relationship between race and spiritual orientation?

Coincidental or/and statistical.

2. Do you see a difference between Native (of Indian culture) religion and native (of the land) spirituality?

Yes. Any religious culture will tend to be more cohesive and more restrictive than any experiential spirituality.

3. Do you think that "core shamanism" can replace or be a useful adjunct to cultural shamanism?

I don't really know, but my simple mind says there should be room for everyone's path/way/perspective. Sometimes people get confused about the difference between being "offended" (which is our own fault) and being "hurt" (which is not).

4. What are your feelings about non-Native use of traditional ceremonial forms? About modification or culturally based changes in those forms by non-Natives?

As a spiritual anarchist I feel that any form can be used when there is understanding, and no form should be used without it. Forms are a means to an end.

5. Do you think the popularization (and commercialization) of shamanism has had a negative effect on Native communities?

The popularization and commercialization of *anything* tends to trivialize it. The trivialization of shamanism has a negative effect on shamanism, not just on Native communities.

6. As a non-Native, have you experienced racial bias that obstructed (or attempted to obstruct) your spiritual work?

Nothing direct. But all racial bias obstructs my work.

7. Do you feel that non-Natives should adopt traditional taboos as part of their involvement with shamanism?

I don't think people should adopt taboos at all, except about hurting themselves or others.

8. How do you feel about Native ceremonies being opened to attendance or participation by non-Natives?

That would be fine but not necessary.

9. Do you think that ceremonial forms such as sweat lodge, vision quest, and shamanic drumming are cross-cultural, or are they particular only to Native cultures and their global correlates?

Cross-cultural, though they are flavored by the matrix in which they occur.

10. *Do you feel personally free of racial bias or anger?*

Er, yes (looking in all seven directions).

SANDRA INGERMAN

Sandra Ingerman, M. A., C. S. C., is the author of Soul Retrieval *and* Welcome Home. *She is the educational director and an international faculty member of the Foundation for Shamanic Studies, directed by Michael Harner. The material presented here is from a transcribed and edited tape Sandra made for me in response to a list of questions I sent her about core shamanism and her own practice. Also included are quotes from an interview conducted by Cat Saunders and printed in the* New Times *in June 1994.*

I like to see myself as a person who practices shamanism. According to Mircea Eliade, a shaman is a person who journeys outside of time and space in order to contact helping spirits for information. As I see it, core shamanism is where the shamanic practitioner uses the shamanic journey (which is cross-cultural) without borrowing any specific rituals from a specific culture. The shamanic journey is what is core to shamanism all over the world. But I don't like to categorize myself as a core shamanic practitioner, as I have a personal issue with being labeled. Because of this, I would like to answer your questions from my own personal viewpoint based on my own experience of practicing shamanism over the last fifteen years.

My background is counseling. So my interest in shamanism is not so much tied up with anthropology, but rather with how I can use shamanism in the 1990s to work with modern-day issues.

The thing I really love about shamanism is that it allows me to get direct spiritual revelation. There are some people who need a physical teacher—a human being teacher—and there are some people who like to learn from getting their own direct revelation from the spirits. One way is not better than the other; we all have different styles of learning.

Michael Harner has been my mentor, and he gave me the gift of teaching me how to journey. My further education has mostly come through my own work with my power animals and teachers in nonordinary reality.

Soul retrieval was a method I learned from my own power animal. I was working with a client who was trying to clear up a trauma she had suffered at an early age. When I asked my power animal in a journey what would be the best healing method, he showed me how to do a soul retrieval. I thought the spirits had taught me a new method, and it turned out when I started doing research that this method has been used throughout the world by shamans since ancient times.

I tend to be a person who contacts my own helping spirits for spiritual knowledge, and that seems to be the most profound way of learning and working for me. In my opinion, one is called to do spiritual work. In my own work I don't seek people as clients or students. I let people know that my services are available, and those who feel a calling to it come. I think that many people are starting to see that "traditional" models of healing are not as effective as they might want them to be, and so there's a search for what can be added to the models that exist in our modern-day culture.

I find today that people experience themselves as being cut off from nature. Modern technology takes us away from the cycles of nature as well as from nature itself. Learning how to journey is a step toward reestablishing that connection. The shamanic journey also provides direct revelation of the spiritual realms for people so that they don't have to go through an intermediary. That is attractive to people in this culture who feel a need to get their own information and take their own power back.

A shamanic practitioner is someone who practices spiritual methods of healing and divination. There has to be a desire from a person to want to go into that realm of working.

I have not had any direct feedback about how Native shamans feel about my work. A lot of Native Americans have come to my workshops and to my practice. I have worked with people from the Crow, Sioux, Apache, Navajo, Pueblo, Penobscot, Cherokee, and Mohawk nations. I know there have been people from other native communities, but the above-mentioned are what come to my mind for now. I have felt good about my work with people from Native communities, and I have never received any negative feedback to date.

I see shamanism as distinct from psychotherapy. In shamanism you are dealing with the spiritual aspect of illness. A shaman takes a shamanic journey into nonordinary reality for helping information. I think that shamanism works well as an adjunct to psychology, but I would not classify them as the same.

I teach people how to contact the spirits through shamanic journeying. Many of the people I teach never use these methods on behalf of another person. They are using this method for their own spiritual development, for their own spiritual growth, for their own personal healing and their own personal evolution.

I think that those who use shamanic journeying on behalf of others have a gift and calling to do this work. I don't train people to be shamans. I can't do that. That is between the person and the spirits themselves. I'm learning my own shamanic path myself. I teach shamanic methods that I have found to work well dealing with modern-day illnesses and problems. It is the role of the shamanic practitioner to practice these methods and perfect the method for himself or herself. If you really embark on this path to practice shamanism, it's something you get spiritual guidance with. What is really important is the result of your work. Does your shamanic work help other people, and do you get consistent positive feedback from those you work with? There are always people whom you might not be able to help, but generally what kind of feedback one gets is the most important question.

People who have the gift, who do have the calling, are usually wounded healers. In our society today I think there are many wounded healers because of the hardship of life. Suffering in life teaches people to be compassionate, which I feel is one of the most important elements in doing healing work. Many people I meet have been in contact with the spiritual realms since they were very young because they didn't have parents and communities that raised them in healthy, loving ways. A lot of the people I work with in soul retrieval were really raised by their own helping spirits and have memories of that.

There's a lot of controversy around how much training a person needs. Yes, practice is important, and I'll be practicing for the rest of my life. But the bottom line is that you either have the gift or you don't. It's good to keep in mind that it could take years for someone to realize the calling and for the world of nonordinary reality to open up. Once a person starts practicing, she must be brutally honest about her own work and in watching the results of her work.

Part of shamanism is about understanding the cycles of nature. The more a shamanic practitioner can get in touch with the cycles of nature, the more she can understand the power that's available. It is very important for people's physical lives to be integrated with the natural world. I also think it's important for shamanic practitioners to take care of their own bodies so that they have a strong instrument to work with.

In core shamanism, we're taking principles that are cross-cultural. It is the responsibility of the people who are studying this to add our own particular ceremonies and rituals. We need to develop a richness without borrowing from some other culture or imitating their ceremonies. The imitations have no power because the ceremonies aren't from our own cultural root. We have to come up with our own ceremonies to augment our practices, to add the depth to our work that ritual and ceremony usually bring.

I think that the most important thing is *practice*. People in our culture seem to want spiritual enlightenment very quickly. We're not always willing to go through the discipline. All spiritual practices are disciplines. Shamanism is a discipline. It's something you do for life. It is said that you never become a shaman; you are always *learning* to become a shaman.

People need to have patience. We must be willing to do the discipline and to do the practice. Then, over time, you can start to notice the *quality* of information you receive when you are in a very deep place of talking with Spirit. Over time, you can also watch the results of using this information. Last of all, it's important to notice whether or not there is any judgment attached to the information you receive, because from a spiritual standpoint, there is no judgment. Things just *are*.

I think that whenever you're creating anything, you're expressing your soul. The creative process involves putting yourself out to the world and shining your own light. This is a very vulnerable thing! In this culture we grew up being judged and graded. We were graded for our art, our writing, our singing, our music. What we learned was that every time you express your soul, or express yourself, there will be a grade. Somebody will judge you. I think this has discouraged people in this culture from expressing themselves freely, because we don't want to be graded.

However, if we can break through this fear and access our willingness to be vulnerable—without worrying about the reaction—then we can move into our birthright. I'm really clear about this: it is our birthright to express our souls.

MEDICINE HAWK WILBURN

I am a coauthor of American Indian Ceremonies *and* Thunderhead: The Life and Times of a Half-Breed, *as well as three other incidental books. I hold B. S., M.Ed., and Ph.D. degrees in education and teach part-time at Chapman University, Riverside Community College, San Bernadino Valley College, and Crafton Hills College. Mainly, however, I teach the sixth grade and after-school Indian crafts. I have three children, Liesl, Rhiannon, and Raymond Judah. I live in San Bernadino, California, with my "feminist, chip-on-the shoulder significant other" and even more children.*

1. How do you see the relationship between race and spiritual orientation?

How long ago were we all one race? Not long, according to the chronology of the earth. The relationship between race and spiritual orientation does not exist; we who live together (birds of a feather—not races) do the same things. The Cherokees (and many other tribes) had blacks, whites, breeds, etc., within their ranks (Wilma Mankiller herself is a "breed"), yet they all practiced pretty much the same religion because they lived in the same place. So the relationship is between geography and people—not races and spirituality.

2. Do you see a difference between Native (of Indian culture) religion and native (of the land) spirituality?

No—see #1. The Celts and Teutons, for instance, with their complex spiritualities, were the "Indians" of Europe (as were many other semi-indigenous groups). It's all geography, again.

3. Do you think that "core shamanism" can replace or be a useful adjunct to cultural shamanism?

There is no cultural shamanism. Core shamanism is the only game in town.

4. What are your feelings about non-Native use of traditional ceremonial forms? About modification or culturally based changes in those forms by non-Natives?

To say that only full-blood (no such thing) Natives can practice a particular spiritual path is tantamount to saying only the original residents of Rhode Island are allowed to be Baptists (because Roger Williams started it all there). At what point did a particular "native race" (a total misnomer) become sole practitioners of a particular spiritual path to the exclusion of all others? What were they doing before that watershed? Were they spiritually exclusive, then? Spirituality of all types should be free to all. If some individual plays God and decides who is worthy, he stands in judgment of *all*. Regardless of age, training, or any other qualifications, this is not enough. One's own heart is the judge of who is qualified to worship in any tradition she chooses. Let's not make any of these "Native spiritual paths" justification for racism, nor even exclusion. Let's not make our religions into racial country clubs that allow only the select elite of a group. A million or so years ago we were *all* (white supremacists, KKK, Aryan Nation, and every other group of questionable and unquestionable humanity) running around in the Olduvai Gorge with nappy heads and black skin. Let's not get uppity about racial and religious exclusion. *My* high priest is Dr. Martin Luther King, Jr.

5. Do you think the popularization (and commercialization) of shamanism has had a negative effect on Native communities?

If you are afraid that a false form of your religion is going to harm your religion in any way, then there is something wrong with your religion.

6. As a métis, have you experienced racial bias that obstructed (or attempted to obstruct) your spiritual work?

Yes. Individuals claiming to be a part of the American Indian Movement repeatedly threatened my life and physically attacked me (twice with knives, once with firearms, which were discharged) before many witnesses, causing me great physical, mental, and emotional distress and pain in the late 1980s. They did this because I taught the spirituality of my mixed-blood tribe to whites and women, and because I gave the sacred pipe to women and placed them in leadership positions. Terrorists claiming to be part of this organization continue to slander and libel me (even those who have never met me) and threaten me to the point that I have not made my residence public knowledge for the last five years, even though I am no longer in any leadership position. I'd say these folks are pretty insecure about their religions (if they have any), their lives, and their hearts.

7. Do you feel that non-Natives should adopt traditional taboos as part of their involvement with shamanism?

Only if you feel in your heart that it is part of your personal spiritual path. For instance, in Santeria, during an initiation the priest/ess divines something for the initiate to abstain from in the following year, which is particular to their saint. Apples are sacred to one saint. Often the initiate is told not to eat them for a year in honor of her saint. If you feel in your heart you should do this as part of your spiritual path, you should, whether it involves shamanism or not.

9. Do you think that ceremonial forms such as sweat lodge, vision quest, and shamanic drumming are cross-cultural, or are they particular only to Native cultures and their global correlates?

Obviously cross-cultural. Anyone knows these rites are almost completely universal.

10. Do you feel personally free of racial bias or anger?

No. I am shallow and unforgiving with general groups who force their beliefs on others by any means.

3

LOOKING WITHIN:
CONTEMPLATIONS ON RACE

THE MIRROR OF ANCESTRY

Look into a mirror, seeking reflections in your face and body of your racial or ethnic ancestry. Look with neither pride nor shame, just with curiosity and acceptance.

What do you associate with these physical characteristics?
How have you felt about them at different times in your life?
How do you think your ancestors felt about their appearance?
What descriptive words for these attributes have you heard that were hurtful?
What words that praised?
What words are your reality?

You carry a legacy in your body. How can this be honored? What needs to be let go of in your thinking in order for you to move with this legacy in beauty?

Visualize a luminous strand of DNA. See yourself and all your ancestors as part of this double helix. Remember all the ancestors you've known or seen pictures of, all part of this shining strand. If you have children or grandchildren, see them also, all connected. Feel the current of life that flows through this strand and the unique gifts it carries. Offer thanks for the good that is within this.

WALKING IN ANOTHER'S MOCCASINS

Visualize yourself as a person of another race. Imagine the differences in appearance and experience. See "yourself" and "your people" (of another race) at a time in history when that race was prospering in isolation from other races. What is life like? How does this feel?

Now see "yourself" and "your people" at a time in history when there is conflict between races and "your people" are not prospering. What is life like and how does this feel?

See "yourself" and "your people" in present time. What is life like? How have the cumulative experiences of history informed the current situation and current feeling?

Imagine meeting "yourself" (the actual you meeting the other-racial you).

How does race affect your interaction?

What are the feelings on either side?

Who is most uncomfortable?

Who controls how the encounter unfolds?

What is the most important thing to communicate?

Return wholly to yourself.

Did this exercise make you feel more or less understanding of other races?

In what ways could you change your attitudes and behaviors in order to be in better relationship with others?

How does your racial prejudice manifest itself; in what thoughts, images, or reactions?

What do you envy about other races? What do you dislike?

What do you wish you knew about other races?

Where do your attitudes come from?

Where does your information come from?

Do you have any friendships or associations with people of other races?

Are any of these relationships truly color blind?

Do you think this is possible? Desirable?

What is your vision of racial harmony?

Have you ever discussed it with a person of another race?

Have you ever asked for that person's vision?

THE BIG CEREMONY

If you are non-Native, imagine yourself the only non-Native at a traditional Native ceremony. If you are Native, imagine yourself at an unfamiliar ceremony of another tribe. There are many people present and the occasion is very important, very holy.

See yourself participating in the ceremony and making terrible blunders, totally disgracing yourself. What do the specifics you imagine in the worst-case scenario reveal about your fears and vulnerabilities?

Look carefully at what underlies the drama you mentally enacted.

Now see yourself participating impeccably at this ceremony, eliciting much admiration and respect from everyone there. What are the details of this enactment? What desires, hopes, needs, and fantasies are part of this scenario? What do they tell you about yourself?

Look at these feelings—the fears and the wishes—and what part they play in your spiritual or ceremonial work. Look at how they influence your involvement with other races, cultures, or communities. How are you using ceremonial occasions to hide from or to capitalize on your personality? Your race? Your tribe? What is your path of honesty and healing in relation to cultural spirituality?

ALIGNMENT

Meditate on your local habitat, on the forms life takes in your environment. In your mind move across the surface of this environment watching, listening, touching, smelling, tasting.

What is the mosaic of life here?
What adjectives describe it?
How well do you know this habitat?

Move below the surface and experience the belowground life of your habitat.

What is the land dreaming?
What do you find in this realm?
How often have you attended to its pulse and secrets?

Move to the upper world, the airs above ground. Fly high and see your region from birds' eyes. Take in the larger perspective and see the patterns of life in their extending webs. Feel the life of the sky.

Do you feel at home here?
What is distinct about your particular habitat?
What is its prevailing medicine?

Ponder your place in this web, your impact, your giveaway, your needs.

What is your commitment here?
How clear is your awareness of relationship?
What sort of partnership do you perceive? What sort of role do
     you play?

Now go deeper. Instead of being a witness and coparticipant, become the habitat itself. Be the body, mind, heart, and spirit of the land and sky. Experience this expansion of consciousness. Begin to understand the differences between stewardship, partnership, and union. The first realizes responsibility, the second participates in respectful kinship, and the third recognizes self. Consider how differently each of these perspectives informs spiritual work and alignment. Consider which of these perspectives is the basis for your own work.

USING ESTABLISHED FORMS

Call to mind a ceremonial form that you use, whether it is sweat lodge, medicine rattles, Native songs, Sun Dance, or whatever. Go back to the first time you used this and to what prompted that experience. Relive that experience.

What were your thoughts, feelings, and physical responses?
How much did you know about the form and its prior uses?
Who introduced it to you?
What unfolded from that initial experience?

Follow that path to your present use of the form.

How has your work with it changed?
How has it changed you?
What do you know now that is different from or more than
    what you knew before?
Have your ever discussed or demonstrated your use of this form
    with Native medicine people?
Have you ever seen a Native use this form?
If so, how did this affect your relationship with the form?
What are you trying to accomplish by using this form?
Is it the only form appropriate to those purposes?
What does its energy connect you to?
What does your energy connect it to?
Is it truly useful for your time, place, and application?
Do you feel a need for permission to use this form? Why? Why not?

Align yourself deeply with this form in order to address its governing spirits. Seek clarity and understanding of your right relationship with this form.

RELIGIOUS HERITAGE

In your thoughts explore the structures and teachings of your family's religious heritage.

Is there continuity in this heritage? Branchings? Breakaways?
How far back does this path lead?
What is your part in it?

Imagine yourself standing at the pulpit or altar of your childhood place of worship to address the congregation.

What would you say? What emotions are present?

Imagine yourself conversing with the founder of that religion. What would you ask? What would you suggest?

Imagine your first ancestors to choose this path of religion.

What drew them?

What resonated?

What needs did it meet?

How have things changed since then?

How do you feel about how their choices affected your life?

Address the deity of this religion (or an aspect of the deity that has most strongly touched your life). Express your desire to either release, deepen, or maintain your connection with your religious heritage. Open to the best way of doing this and of being at peace with your choices.

RECOGNITION OF SUFFERING

Recall or visualize a situation where you were confronted by a hostile response from a person of another race. Go through the sequence of words, motions, and energies that unfolded in that situation. Observe your mental, emotional, and physical states in their shifts, and how they informed your participation in the situation.

Now go through the sequence with recognition of the other person's shifting states. Look deeply into the language of voice, posture, gesture, expression, and movement and find the clues to that person's hostility. Recognize the fear and pain behind anger and hatred. Realize the suffering that leads to hostility and violence.

Without judgment toward yourself or the other person, fill yourself now with compassion. Feel how compassion could change the situation you are recalling or visualizing. Get a sense of different ways interracial tensions, misunderstandings, and confrontations could be dealt with if surface emotions were not what guided people's actions.

PART TWO

GENDER

4

REFLECTIONS ON GENDER

A young Cheyenne man on his way home from participating in a Sun Dance stopped at our place to attend a sweat. The Sun Dancer was courteous as he sat with us around the fire watching the rocks heat. He directed all his conversation and questions toward my husband—who often fire-tended but never conducted sweats—and ignored me, the ceremonial leader. It was obvious that his behavior had nothing to do with discretion. He simply dismissed me because of my gender. He even offered tobacco to my husband rather than to me.

I was not offended or upset but let the sweat take its natural course. It turned out to be a particularly hot and long ceremony, owing to the large number of attendees and the spiritual needs of the occasion. The Sun Dancer had the most difficulty of anyone with the heat but afterward expressed appreciation for how the sweat had been conducted.

In town several nights later my husband and I encountered the Cheyenne on the street and stood talking with him for a while. Before parting the young man apologized to me, saying he really hadn't thought before the sweat that I could "do it" and that he'd been wrong. I wished him well, grateful for his honesty and youthful openheartedness. At least he had taken the opportunity to sweat and had experienced something that would perhaps broaden his perspectives. Too rarely does openheartedness supersede prejudice.

In discussing gender issues I want to make clear that I am not criticizing Native culture. What I'm addressing is a pervasive trend in the "natural" Spirituality movement to divide men's and women's spiritual natures. This trend seems to me as unfortunately convenient and insufficiently examined as the division of spirituality along racial lines.

If one peruses a list of well-known medicine women—names such as Brooke Medicine Eagle, Twylah Nitsch, Dhyani Ywahoo, Wabun Wind, and so on—it becomes apparent that these capable people are known at least as much for their teachings about "women's spirituality" as for their work simply as medicine people. On the other hand, a comparable list of men—Wallace Black Elk, Brant Secunda, Rolling Thunder, Archie Fire Lame Deer, and so on—are not usually thought of as representing "men's spirituality," but as representative of medicine work in general. Perhaps this discrepancy is part of the reason some women are drawn more to core shamanism, with its nongendered practices. I've noticed, when I'm on the road teaching, that people often assume I must be offering workshops or sweats for women only, though the lecture topics or ceremonial intentions certainly don't invite that assumption.

The excellent teachings oriented to "women's spirituality" coming from such people as Brooke Medicine Eagle, Susun Weed, and others are really teachings for all people. They are insights centered in a perspective that is accessible to all of us—not merely to the "female part" of ourselves, but to the spirit. That women, with their experiences of menstruation, childbirth, and caregiving, have been the ones to identify and bring forth these truths of spirit does not make the truths themselves feminine.

In the teachings of the "blood mysteries" has been a path of awareness and deepening for women that for men has had to come about, if at all, through different life experiences. Though the paths of men and women sometimes differ in this regard, the ultimate understandings can be the same. Sharing the teachings between genders may hasten the reaching of mutual understandings, and if teachings are not labeled "men's" or "women's," it will be easier for them to be recognized as vital for all. If spirituality, as opposed to religion or culture, has no color, it must also have no sex.

Men and women have much to share with each other from their various experiences. First they need a context for examining and understanding these experiences. Sometimes that context comes from someone older or more awakened, and this person may also need to be someone of a like gender. Once understanding has emerged, sharing can extend to the larger community, and it is at this point that I feel that assigning gender to the teachings is a hindrance. Truth is not feminine or masculine. Feminizing God into Goddess, masculinizing Goddess into God, or even personifying the Mystery at all is a process of culture, religion, or personal orientation, not of spirit. The attributes associated with deity are not masculine or feminine except in their relationship to conditioned outlook.

Some teachers have been given guidance or directives toward working with gender duality in its polarized perspective. My own spiritual imperative, reinforced by the vision and skills I've been given, is to offer reminders of the path of completeness. I work not in opposition but in addition to other teachers, all of us within the sacred dream of healing.

I do not ignore what the women's spirituality movement has brought about through its emergence in the modern world; indeed, I honor it and have at times participated in its dance. The feelings and hungers that have been satisfied by spiritually focused gatherings of women, whether in print or in person, have been tremendous gifts to a troubled society. Women's voices, their very thoughts and visions, have been long suppressed. As these voices are finally freed from fear and restriction, and their natural strength, clarity, and wisdom renewed, it is important not to confine their messages.

Putting an emphasis on gender is akin to dwelling on the fact that in the northern hemisphere water spins one way down a drain while in the southern hemisphere it spins the opposite way, while ignoring that what is happening in both cases is water flowing down the drain. The spin that gender may put on life's experiences is only one aspect of consciousness. As human beings we have the potential to flow in any direction we choose and to attune to whatever "spin" brings us growth and realization of wholeness.

A medicine man once told me he was sending a woman to me for instruction on the "women's way" with the pipe. I never figured out what he expected me to tell her. My use of the pipe was based on what my teacher, Lewis, had demonstrated and on what I had learned through interaction with the pipe itself and with pipe carriers. I don't know any "women's way."

Some years ago I was asked to co-conduct a pipe ceremony for a man with cancer. The other pipe was carried by a visiting ceremonialist and healer who had been trained by several venerable Native medicine men. We sat side by side, laying out our medicine tools before beginning the ceremony. Our assortment of objects was almost identical. We each filled our pipes and prayed, and again our ways were similar. At the end of the ceremony the healer remarked that though he had been given extensive training in pipe ceremonies, his own way had evolved over the years and was different from that of his teachers. I told him that my work had followed a similar course of change. It was remarkable how alike our ceremonies and use of sacred objects were. To me, the pipe is the pipe, the lodge is the lodge, the individual is the individual, and the medicine is the medicine. There is no men's or women's way.

It is easy to assign gender to spirituality because men and women have become so deeply cleft. A mind-set that is thousands of years old has created an appearance of inherently differing attributes and capacities. But are they inherent? If variations to the gender "rules" are counted and the insidious impact of societal dictates are examined, then the categorizations begin to look more like conditioning than inherencies. If you question the generalizations of race, you should also reconsider the lines drawn between the sexes.

Having seen numerous exceptions to every gender stereotype, I believe that what many people are discerning is not truly inherent capacity but conditioned propensity. These are two very different things. To say that many women have a conditioned propensity to act in thus-and-such gender-specific way is not the same as believing that women are naturally defined by that propensity. This is true whether those propensities are regarded as positive, negative, or neutral. To see something as conditioning gives us impetus and room to change that conditioning and grow.

Biology as destiny is not only a narrow view but also an invalidating one to those whose biology is different from what is considered normal. The complexities of each individual's dance with chemistry and biology is too manipulatively and superficially dealt with when physical processes are used to define spiritual identity. The "evidence" is too glib to be trustworthy, and too incomplete as well.

To say that men and women are different is to voice the obvious, yet it doesn't necessarily follow that men and women should divide themselves spiritually. It is equally valid to say that individuals are different—so much so that a certain man and a certain woman may have more in common than that man and another man, or that woman and another woman. When you consider how vital, how crucial to survival and well-being is the mutuality of men and women, then it follows that if separations are to be made, they should be according to less alienating differences than those of sex.

The more the sexes are perceived through the measure of differences—real or imposed, biological or conditioned—the more excuses men and women find not to understand or accept one another. Suppose a teacher divided a classroom of children: boys on one side, girls on the other, and a wide aisle between. (This is really not hard to imagine.) Now, instead, suppose the teacher put Caucasians on one side and African Americans on the other, or children of single-parent households on one and those of dual-parent households on the other—or made the division according to whether the children are of urban or rural backgrounds.

Whatever the division, it will affect how the children relate to each other; it will also affect the classroom's dynamic and the children's self-images. Division is a potent message. Further, suppose a partition is placed between the two groups, and the teacher uses different texts and different teachings to instruct the groups of children. The group with urban backgrounds, for instance, receives education about cities and city society, and the rural group learns about farms. It is easy to see how this takes an actual difference and turns it into separation and limitation. It is easy to see how this impedes understandings from being developed and shared and binds individuals to narrow, incomplete visions of self and society. It is easy to see how this could create adversariness.

It is not only women who need to understand the historical background of women's experience and to give birth to a transformation that validates courage, self-respect, and fulfillment. It is not only men who need to realize the suffering in historical male self-oppression and to emerge into realigned priorities. The partition needs to come down, the people to mingle, and the teachings to be heard and used by all. I'm not suggesting that women and men try to become the same; I'm praying that women and men, together, become free, mutually aware human beings.

Oft-heard statements from people engaged in "natural" spirituality:

> "Men need more purification than women."
> "Men are attuned to the sun; women to the moon."
> "Women are more intuitive than men."
> "Women are more in touch with their emotions than are men."
> "Men are the protectors; women are the life bringers."
> "Men are Sky energy; women are Earth energy."
> "Men are projective; women are receptive."

Generalizations such as these are easily justified using a model of duality that ignores a diversity of individual truths. This model of complementary opposites can be tidy and satisfying as a basis for perception and relationship.

People sometimes insist that they are referring to male and female "energies" rather than male and female persons when they apply this system of duality. In practice, however, it comes out that "female energy" means women and the stereotypical attributes associated with women, and "male energy" means men and the stereotypical attributes associated with men. I hear some men talking about their "female energy" as if it were a pair of sunglasses they used in specialized circumstances, or women referring to their "male energy" as if it were something located in the back of their closets. It comes across as a sort of multiple personality disorder, or a profound yet artificial fragmentation of self. Where do men get their "female energy" and women their "male energy"? At what percentage point do some women have enough "male energy" to qualify for doing "male" things? This whole notion seems peculiarly frustrating.

Sex differences are viewed from three perspectives: body chemistry and reproductive anatomy, role conditioning, and natural correspondences. All three are questionable foundations for spiritual dogma. No two human bodies, even those of twins, are exactly alike. The complex interplay of mind and body, nature and nurture, emotions and chemistry, experience and genetics, is in constant motion and change. Hormones are in shifting balances; the grace of possibility is ever present within the body as it responds to everything around it. The temptation to reduce all of this to gender formulas is urged by a need for an orderly sense of understanding and control with which to guide relationships. It is a need for definition: this is what a man is; this is what a woman is; this is what I am. It is an establishment of existence, a position in the tangible universe in terms that are recognizable or shared by others. It is something to hold on to and use as a basis for comparison. For some people it is a core from which to extend and explore; for others it is simply a mind-set, rigid and surrounded by doubt and isolation.

You can look at a body and say "this is female" or "this is male," but what does that really imply about spiritual capacity? In talking about "female energy" in terms of biology you must consider the body of the lean, nonmenstruating athlete, the body of the pregnant or lactating mother, the body of the low-estrogen elder, the body of the young girl, and all other variations of female form present in this world, with all their descriptive "energies." Male biological diversity must take into account boys, teens, celibates, tantric practitioners, elders, meditators, soldiers, and so on, each having different energetic balances and functional priorities within their inherent organic paradigm. "Normal" physiology can include a lively range of "energies" for both sexes.

The second perspective used to define sex differences is role conditioning, and this is still underestimated when examining gender issues. As a midwife I was present at the earliest stages of many human lifetimes. I worked with parents who were rich, middle-class, poor, educated, illiterate, countercultural, mainstream, of many races and religions: a parental potpourri. It was astonishing how pervasively and immediately sex role conditioning was imposed on babies, across the board.

The idea that boys will be boys and girls will be girls according to stereotypes is taught to children from the very first, perhaps even prenatally. Children are not born into cultural freedom of selfhood. The words I heard parents greet their newborns with were often words unconsciously instructing the children in certain roles as males and females. Even if the words were playful ("Isn't she a looker?" "He's got the shoulders of a football player," "Grabbing for the breast already, isn't that just like a boy," "Look at her pout, she'll get what she wants from Daddy every time"), they transmitted beliefs about self to very receptive, newly arrived consciousnesses.

The first thing most people wanted to know about a child was its sex. "It's a baby" was the standard midwife's reply. What would happen if at birth newborns were welcomed by hearing "I love you; I'm so glad you're here!" instead of "It's a boy!" or "It's a girl!"?

By school age children are firmly ensconced in the gender roles reinforced by school, church, TV, and other media, and by the examples of conditioned adults and other children. It is a relentlessly efficient indoctrination. Feminist schoolteachers were appalled at viewing videotapes of their performances in the classroom. It was observed that the teachers favored boys over girls: gave them more attention, more feedback, more latitude, more recognition, and more encouragement. And these were the feminist teachers.

As a mother with a (now adult) son, I know it doesn't have to be this way. A child raised by someone who doesn't believe—and doesn't live—the gender stereotypes has more freedom of self-image and expression. It is always funny when people admire my son and say how much they wish their children could be like him, yet when I mention the precepts my parenting is based on their interest wanes. It is easier to perpetuate ingrained patterns than to question shadow-ridden societal and personal beliefs. TV, toys of violence to the Earth and to others, gender role conditioning, public schools, disrespectful relationships, and other features of modern child rearing are considered normal or at best unavoidable. To challenge this complacence takes a clarity of belief but not as much of a struggle as people imagine. If you see something as normal, then of course it will be difficult to alter it, because you'd be fighting your own belief. To see an alternative as normal, as natural, is to acknowledge your own view of reality. Either way, it can be done, but its ease or difficulty is a mirror of where your beliefs abide.

As men and women increasingly envision themselves in nontraditional roles and then manifest lives that expand society's vision in turn, people begin to accept a larger sense of what the categories male and female can encompass. Warrior, shaman, merchant, builder, trickster, judge, nurturer, healer, artist, teacher, all those archetypes that used to be embodied exclusively through one sex or the other are now more easily seen as options for either—and as options, not identities. Wildness, nurturance, sensuality, wisdom, and so on don't belong to maleness or femaleness but are part of a spectrum available for expression in the individual's life, in individual ways.

As long as gender duality rules our thinking, vision will be blocked. If career work takes male energy and child rearing takes female energy, the househusband will always feel at risk for losing his masculinity and the businesswoman for losing her femininity. The fearful belief remains that engaging too strongly with a "part" of you that is not your biological category will endanger your image among peers, your place in society, and your sense of gender identity. If nurturance always connotes the feminine and can't simply be nurturance—a thing unto itself—then nurturant men will always wonder if they are real men. Non-nurturant men will continue to have an excuse for their immaturity, and overnurturant women will continue to believe they are fulfilling their biological imperative. Thinking of energies and qualities in gender terms encumbers them with implications that sabotage our freedom, happiness, and self-acceptance.

This leads us to the third perspective, that of natural correspondences: Father Sky, Mother Earth; Grandfather Sun, Grandmother Moon; male rain (the hard kind), female rain (the soft kind); Grandfather Peyote, Grandmother Sweetgrass; lightning as male, ocean as female; and so on.

Alignment with natural powers is meant to be an act of connectedness and enlargement of self. Personification through gender designations is a way of naming kinship and establishing relatedness, of expressing respectful intimacy. It should be remembered, however, that not all cultures perceive these relationships the same way. In some cultures the moon is seen as male and the sun as female, for example (or both are seen as female). Such personification can suffer from the same lack of flexibility that characterizes all constrictive beliefs.

Rigid dualizing reinforces "otherness" based on sex, and in our world, otherness is the repository for projective fears. These isolating fears are the root of violence of all kinds—mental, emotional, and physical. The mirror of self will always be fragmented if otherness precludes instead of reflects wholeness. There will always be blame, always be a need for self-defense. How will men and women ever trust each other and accept a fullness of responsibility and possibility, ever truly love each other, if locked in isolating definitions? How will we ever know what a human being can become?

At the Native spirituality gathering in Canada that I described in chapter 1, a large area was established where women could spend time or camp. There was a moon lodge and a tepee for councils. The area was cordoned off and no men were allowed in.

The area had a lovely feel to it. You could see women brushing each other's hair, singing, doing crafts, working and chatting together. You could hear soft drumming, smell wonderful foods cooking, and see the women in their colorful, graceful clothing walking across the meadow or laughing around their fires. It seemed an idyllic place where one could be nurtured, appreciated, and given a sense of safety and acceptance.

The men responded to it in two ways. The first was to express pleasure at this display of separate womanliness. Some men felt more manly when seeing women enacting roles as strong but handily secluded entities. The other reaction was a mixture of wistfulness, envy, and resentment. Men could see how *nice* the women's area was, and they were envious. They uncaringly scheduled ceremonies to conflict with women's activities. They saw no reason to include women as principle participants in group ceremonies other than in "female," token, or adjunct roles. After all, the women had their own area where they could listen to "women's" teachings, conduct "women's" ceremonies, and do "women's" medicine.

Some of the men wanted to set up a "sun lodge" as "balance" to the moon lodge: the exclusive clubhouse syndrome. There was no impetus toward dealing with issues of control, representation, spiritual hypocrisy, or sexually abusive behaviors. After all, the women had their place so should be satisfied, as though separation in itself was some sort of honoring or solution.

Is this a model for healthy society, for women to have their own place so that the world can continue to avoid addressing the causes of violence and suffering? I understand women's need for safe places, healing places, private places, and men's need for supportiveness and meaningful connections with their gender peers. But when these needs obscure the more crucial need for mutuality in healing and connectedness and obstruct the individual's freedom to move transformatively, then priorities should be reconsidered in the light of greater well-being.

There is a tendency to get stuck in patterns of response that at one time were useful but eventually become outgrown. Because of our history, there was a time when gender-exclusive consciousness raising and solidarity was helpful (and for some people a matter of survival). For that to open the way for actual change of the systemized violence and despair in our world, a partnership must be formed. The more deeply entrenched the image and experience of otherness, the harder it is to walk together. Anything that perpetuates those irreconcilabilities—whether it is always calling the Great Mystery "Grandfather," or not allowing women to drum at peyote meetings, or assuming that men can't control their behavior—should be reexamined if it doesn't further spiritual maturity and healing.

I don't see myself in the popular Jungian view, as a woman having "male energy" or a "male side" auxiliary to my female persona.* I see myself as an embodied awareness experiencing life on Earth. That experience includes attunement to many nongendered energies expressed in many forms. There is an aspect that is for me physically female but never severed from a freedom of consciousness that

---

* Jung's anima and animus seem little more than a mystical version of Freud's division of the mind into ego, superego, and id—that is, they remain abstract projections, not truly integrated into the self. The animus is a masculine "part"; but if society doesn't recognize women's ability or right to do masculine things, then how does a woman ever relate to her animus as a natural aspect of her self?

The Jungian model, from what I understand, is a dualistic system with an ultimate goal of alchemized wholeness. In this it reminds me of communism with its ultimate withering away of dictatorship. In practice neither the wholeness nor the withering away ever seems to happen: there's too much invested in the status quo.

identifies self and others simply as sacred being. Moon, Earth, Sky, sweetgrass, man, woman; the truth of each is addressed as sacred being.

The ancient concept of a dual universe is not discarded through wholeness. All the traditional pairings of male/female, light/dark, life/death, and so on can be useful for developing teachings of balance, harmony, and order.

Duality can be a mirror that reveals hidden completion. It can be a way of dynamic interaction within balance and equality. It can be an alchemy, a participation in creativity, love, and the ecstasy of union. This alchemy has been sadly distorted through the ages, however, to become a divisiveness, where instead of union there is competition, oppression, narrow-mindedness, alienation, and skewed values. The honoring has become an aberrant dislocation of truth, and the pairings have become opponents. Instead of a mirror there is a wall of belief; clarity and cooperation are impaired. What was meant to enlarge understanding has been put in service of contraction. Ecstasy has be replaced by mistrust and perversity.

To experience grandfather/grandmother, father/mother, brother/sister, male/female as balance and celebrations within beauty, both their connotations and worldly realities must be brought into healthy relationship. Until this happens, concepts of duality will be weighted with the suffering and denial of equality carried by men and women for thousands of years. Much may be renewable from the ancient mandala, but until minds, hearts, and bodies are cleared of the patterns of violation and adversity, I say let it go. What is true will endure. Let spiritual language and practice be free of gender so we can dream a new dream together. Let duality once again become a transcendent path to wholeness, not a dogmatic pendulum of separation.

Moving now from the frying pan into the fire, I offer some reflections on menstrual taboos, again in the light of native spirituality, not in judgment of indigenous cultural practices.

The core of my belief about menstruation is that it is each woman's personal and private business what she does while she is menstruating. I have not met a shaman or healer who could tell whether or not I'm having a period (though I've never tried to be deceptive). The power of belief plays a major role in what effect menstruation has on people, objects, and ceremonies.

Of course menstrual "energies" are real, as hormonal-emotional-psychic emanations, but they are shaped and filtered through each woman's totality of consciousness and through the context those energies are given. I've heard the full array of adjectives applied to menstruating women by traditionalists: unfocused, dangerous, overpowering, unclean, indiscriminate, unbalanced—all words that imply lack of control or clarity. Whether couched in terms of specialness or of abhorrence, the underlying belief is a restrictive one.

I see three courses for a menstruating woman in relation to spiritual work with others. First, she can use her knowledge and awareness of self to harmonize her energies with the group's, contributing in whatever way is best to her. Second, she can refrain from group work based on her particular need for solitude. Third, she can ask the group's leader or its members if they are feeling any difficulties with her energies, and respond by realigning or withdrawing.

These three courses are paths of awareness and responsibility worthy of grown women. Not only that, they are worthy of men also, and of women who are not menstruating. Myriad powerful natural energies are at work in people and in the cosmos in general, each with the potential for changing the balances of ceremony or medicine work. There are moon phases, astrological configurations, emotional states, forces of ego, interpersonal dynamics, life changes, weather patterns, and so on. Why is it that menstruation is made the star of the taboo show? Why are powerful ovulation energies discounted? Why are other traditional taboos not given consideration today? Why is there such controversy around this issue?

One possibility is that other taboos (refraining from sex, from particular foods or salt, or from food at all for prescribed, sometimes extended periods of time in preparation for ceremony) are too demanding for the modern, gratification-oriented person. Dare I suggest that we have become lazy and attached to our habits and comforts? It doesn't take much effort to exclude menstruating women from a ceremony. It's an easy taboo that establishes an appearance of traditionality, protocol, and spiritual responsibility. Sensitive adherents to menstrual taboos try to make the excluded women feel honored and distinguished by this exclusion and usually give the ex-cluded women some alternative activity in which to engage. Others may not be so polite, making no bones about their loathing of men-strual blood.

There is much talk of lunar rhythms in relation to menstruation for the "natural" woman. The moon pulls on all fluids, creating flux on many levels—and for all people, not just for menstruating women. My ex-husband used to be insufferably sullen during every new moon and for years did nothing to integrate this. No one would've sug-gested he be excluded from ceremony, but I would rather have sat in ceremony with a dozen fecklessly bleeding women than endured his vibes in a sweat lodge during new moon. But not all women, even "natural" ones, bleed and ovulate in tune with moon cycles.

In talking with hundreds of women as a midwife, I found an amazing variety of responses—physical, emotional, sexual, and psychic—to menstruation. I also found that many women's cycles do not coincide with the moon's, even for those women living without electricity and consciously attending to the moon's light. The length of their cycles, which are either longer or shorter than moon cycles, allows them to experience a slowly shifting alignment of their bleeding and ovulation with all the various phases of the moon. Some of these women speak of how each alignment gives a distinct context to their period. Bleeding during a full moon is a different experience from bleeding during a new moon, for example, and suggests that activities appropriate to one bleeding time might not feel compatible with another bleeding time.

With all these shifting parameters, perhaps it is not useful to dictate what women should be feeling and doing during their menstrual periods. At least, it seems to me that women, who are conditioned by role if not by nature to be sensitive to energies and to the needs of others, should have more say about their actual experiences. It is incongruous to hear someone sitting with his judgments, his own energies perhaps influenced by modifiers such as caffeine, nicotine, junk food, and egotism, telling women about an organic process he can't even detect. This of course does not describe all ceremonial leaders, but it makes the point that there is more to consciousness and to harmonious spiritual presence than just adherence to cultural taboos.

The feeling often conveyed when someone says, "I don't sweat with menstruating women," is disturbingly similar to that which accompanies statements like "I don't share drinking fountains with blacks" or "Only full-bloods should hold sacred bundles." We must be careful with our judgments. The smaller we draw our circles the less medicine they contain.

The bleeding time is a releasing phase in the cycle. The habitat built up in preparation for a possible pregnancy breaks down and is passed out of the uterus during menstruation. This letting go of structure is what is fearful to some ceremonialists, particularly since it involves blood. But is loss of structure really threatening? Retrograde planets, people in the midst of divorce, heyokas, smudge herbs, burning wood, and many other things often present in ceremony are dissolving influences. These energies are transformative. They carry the potential for change and newness. They carry dreams and vision as well as release and clearing. Brought into ceremony in a sacred way, menstrual energies can contribute as harmoniously as any other natural forces.

European shamanic tradition did not specifically exclude menstruating women from mixed-gender ceremonies. The prohibitions followed by many non-Native people in North America are not rooted in their own spiritual heritages. It is one thing to abide by the protocols of a ceremonial leader who requests adherence to those taboos; that is only honest and respectful. It is another to adopt those cultural aspects into one's own spiritual path or to impose them on others just because they invoke an appearance of traditional legitimacy. It is important to explore deeply within one's own beliefs. Abiding by Native taboos is not going to turn anyone into an Indian.

One of the aspects of taboo that needs further pondering is its scapegoating function. This is an important part of the role taboos play in community. When something goes wrong in a ceremony— or in a household, for that matter—it is useful to have something to name as the cause of disorder, something to blame as a reason for malfunction. Identifying a cause and effect frees a situation from lingering unhappiness and psychic malaise. Things become clear-cut and solvable. Taboo violation is made the scapegoat for everything from ceremonial "failure" to leadership incompetency. Personal and tribal misfortune and illness are often traced to taboo violation, thus giving a basis for absolution, healing, and a return to orderliness. The way this serves a tribal society is complex and effective—more subtle than the simplistic explanation given here.

In the present-day United States, however, beliefs are not shared and communities are not tribal. Our melting pot of ethnic backgrounds, religions, family upbringings, and other diverse factors require a different response to problems. The service that taboos provided for tribal societies is not what I see being enacted with their application in contemporary life. Without consensus of belief and a homogenous, supportive community, the use of taboos to diagnose problems and restore harmony causes alienation instead of solution.

All kinds of difficulties and misfortune are blamed on the presence of menstruating women. I've seen malfunctions occur and leaders eagerly look for a menstruating woman to pin them on, though none was present. Using taboos this way makes it easy to avoid looking at deeper or more uncomfortable causes of problems.

Non-Native women in particular have been oppressed by shame-producing societal attitudes about menstruation and other organic female functions. It is not helpful to propagate further negative messages about female bodies. Even when these messages *sound* positive, there is always the shadowed and readily invoked flip side, the shifted language that condemns and controls instead of inquires about a woman's own experience.

I was invited to a ceremony and feast by a traditionally trained, non-Native medicine man. It took place in a private home and was a small gathering of men and women, some Native, most not. I was on the last day of my period, so I brought along my teenage son to represent our family at the ceremony.

Preliminary to the pipe ceremony the medicine man asked all menstruating women to step back from the circle that would be smoking the pipe. Almost all the women stepped back, leaving very few people in the circle. The pipe carrier looked startled and dismayed. "You, too?" he said to me in a baffled tone.

After the pipe ceremony we went to the feasting room, and the medicine man asked me to prepare the "spirit plate" of food. I hesitated and asked if he was sure he wanted me to do that. At his assurance I entered the kitchen, only to be loudly confronted by a Native woman who wanted to know what the hell I was doing in the kitchen while menstruating. She made a scene with the medicine man, who slapped his forehead and exclaimed that he had forgotten that I was in an unclean state of being. I was embarrassed by this commotion and felt a bit misused. It struck home again that this taboo has more to do with belief than with particular energies. I certainly felt "normal" and not in the least unbalanced or dangerous. The medicine man had been so unaffected by my energies as to have forgotten my menstrual state moments after the ceremony ended. Neither of us is Native or were raised with these taboos. As my son commented later on our drive home: "That scene sure felt weird."

Menstruation should not be ignored, nor its potentials discounted. The menstrual time is a reminder to pay attention to your energy. For women in the past, and for many busy women of today, it can be a time for rest, for respecting yourself and your own needs, and for honoring a regular set-aside space for taking stock of inner and outer balances and tending to them. In traditional Native cultures where women were always at work doing tasks for family and tribe, it seems vital that women had a designated time for personal renewal. Many women today lead lives filled to the brim with household preoccupations, career demands, or generally outward-moving energy. Little time is given to simple relaxation, introspection, self-nurturance, and peaceful solitude. It is no wonder that menstrual rituals or observances have again become a focus for spiritual women. They provide a traditional and primal context for self-respect. For some women this gives a justifiable basis for doing something they don't feel motivated enough—or assertive enough—to carry out without that excuse or reminder. With the weight of tradition behind her, a woman can claim a few days each month for her own physical, emotional, mental, and psychic health.

This is a good thing in itself, but I wonder if it would not be even better for women—and other hardworking, caregiving people—to extend the lessons of the "menstrual break" to a deeper, daily level. Attention to balances is something for which our modern life has given most of us more opportunity. With a loosening of gender roles comes a widening of ways in which work can be shared and needs responded to more equally. Attention to balances on a daily basis means that paths are sought that can integrate personal well-being with caregiving of others. It means that awareness of what is needed, and of what is going on, becomes immediate and not attached to a particular formula. These paths have flexibility, an attribute of true response-ability. As a person becomes more sensitive to energy flows and balances, he or she can act upon a growing awareness of what serves health and harmony. It may help to follow someone else's rules or rhythms as attunement develops—personal practices emerge from such teachings—but these are only useful to their degree of alignment with what is natural and right for the individual.

Why limit attention to the menstrual time? Explore, heal, celebrate, and use premenstrual energies, ovulation energies, and postpartum energies (for example). Dance not only with the Moon but with the Earth, the Sun, the stars. Know yourself, and act upon that knowing each day, with respect for yourself and for others.

The last area I'd like to examine here is that of sexual abuse. This subject reaches also into racial and community interactions but seems most appropriately addressed in this part of the book.

I recall being told not to look Native men in the eyes or to ever hug them unless I was interested in sexual intimacy, because these signals would be understood by Native men to imply such interest. Cultural sensitivity is fine, but I know that most Native men aren't living in a vacuum with no interaction with mainstream society. Sexual predation is usually not a case of misread signals but of a need for control.

Stories of Native medicine men and their sexual pursuits are so common as to be ubiquitous. Non-Native teachers are equally notorious. When a teacher commits a sexual abuse of power, the result is confusion and disillusionment that stem from equating knowledge or skill with enlightened behavior. When the teacher is Native and the victim is not, racial guilt often urges violation of personal feelings over offending the representative of an oppressed people.

The misuse of sweat lodges, teaching relationships, and healing situations as opportunities for making sexual advances is not a rare phenomenon. Mixed signals—or even correctly read signals—may sometimes play a part, but that does not change the fact that these are not appropriate venues for seduction.

Despite the knowledge that abuses of power and trust are occurring, people seem at a loss for how to confront them. At risk is the hopeful image of Native medicine men as holy personages. During one of my gatekeeping stints at the Canadian gathering two cars arrived. The first was driven by one of the gathering's principle medicine men, the second by his wife. Both cars held additional occupants, mostly Native.

As I stood answering questions and giving information to the medicine man he reached out and stroked my hair, complimenting me on it. Knowing this man's reputation I was not unduly shocked, though his forwardness in view of his wife caught me by suprise. If I had reached in to caress his hair instead of he mine, there would've been accusations of racial patronization as well as sexual trespass, but as a Caucasian woman I was expected to be at least polite about his unsolicited physical intimacy.

I was not challenged by this situation, but many women, especially those seeking teachers, may encounter the double jeopardy of victim guilt and racial guilt. Women are conditioned to accept blame for "attracting" sexual attention, and as members of the dominant race, many white women are easily entangled in anxieties about obligation. If they are also hungry for spiritual teachings, they may compromise themselves in order not to be turned away. This is not healthy for anyone. It is wrong to demand that women should "know better" or always have the wherewithal to guard themselves from being taken advantage of sexually. On the other hand, it is unrealistic to expect teachers to be fully mature spiritual beings, whatever their race.

It is important to confront abuse and to insist on accountability in ways that promote positive relationships. We need to help each other in this, not isolate those who are struggling or who have made mistakes, and not leave women without recourse.

The position of teacher or medicine person can be isolating in itself, exposed to much comment from others but often not equally accessible to support. It is often difficult for a leader—a spiritual authority, an elder, a teacher—to ask for help, to admit problems, to reveal uncertainty or pain.

Many people use the issue of sexual abuse of power as an argument for why men and women should not ceremonialize together, or why clothing should be worn in the sweat lodge. Are Native spiritual forms now inextricably linked to Christian-influenced beliefs about men, women, and sexuality? Is it beneficial for women to involve themselves with the ceremonies and medicine work of patriarchal medicine men? Where is spirituality's common ground here?

It might help to think in terms of individuals instead of in terms of tradition. Whether or not any of the ways women and men currently ceremonialize together are traditional, the mind-sets of the people definitely are not. We all have been pushed out of "the garden" by society, religion, parental doctrine, or experiences of abuse. The path to a sacred and natural sense of sexuality, nakedness, and respectful inner and outer response to one another is essential for us to discover. In finding this path we need to be honest about where we're at. We need to be considerate and wise. But also we need to cut through both the neopagan platitudes about celebrating the human form and the patriarchal certainty that naked women are the root of all evil.

The wearing or not wearing of clothing does not change basic attitudes. The skyclad ritualist may still have appearance anxiety and shame. The cotton-muffled sweat participant may still be struggling with lecherous urges and distracting speculations. What is needed is more communication, sensitivity, and willingness to envision options that serve the true needs of the times. More spiritual protocols will not help, any more than does more civil legislation, to heal what ails our lives. Women and men need to hear each other. Teachers and shamans need to address what is real.

Learning is always a gift and an expansion. Learning gives resource for choice. It offers guidance and broadens horizons. But spiritual reality comes through authentic connection with the Mystery. How this translates into beliefs and practices for each individual is a process whose compass, when aligned with Spirit, cannot be at odds with the good of all. This work does not manifest in isolation.

In the healing of relations between women and men, and within women and men, will be the healing of life's sacred hoop. In this the children will be blessed, the Earth will be blessed, and sexuality will become an expression of creativity, union, and ecstasy.

The fire of sexuality is present in all medicine work regardless of ceremonial form because it is part of life's primal energy. In learning to move with this power in spiritual ways, male and female reunite not only with each other but with the regenerative source of sacred medicine.

5

PASSING THE TALKING STICK

GREY WOLF

1. Have you ever experienced sexual bias that obstructed (or attempted to obstruct) your spiritual work? If so, how did you respond to it?

There have been attempts to obstruct or influence my spiritual work by those whom I consider to have a sexual bias. In these cases I have explained my attitude. I have honored the territory that I was in to avoid offending those of that territory.

2. What are your beliefs regarding menstrual taboos and women's "moontime"?

I have tried to understand the menstrual taboos and discover the background to them. I feel that the underlying reason is ignorance and fear of that which is not understood: the "mystery" of women's power. Mescaline, the derivative of peyote, raises the blood pressure. If a male has high blood pressure to start with he may well suffer a nose bleed after using peyote. He may not know this, and perhaps would not admit his weakness if he did, and so says "there must be a woman on her moon around."

3. Do you conduct gender-exclusive ceremonies? If so, do these make up the bulk of your work?

I have pretty well stopped leading ceremonies due to poor health, and only once led an all-male sweat. This was a special request by two young men who were preparing for a Sun Dance and who requested a "warrior" sweat. I do not feel that anyone should be excluded unless they are under the influence of consciousness-altering drugs, including alcohol.

4. Do you believe there is an inherent difference in men's and women's spiritual natures, practices, and destinies?

No, I do not believe there is an inherent difference between male and female spiritual natures. I know that there is a conditioned cultural difference. I must confess to a certain amount of sexual bias. I feel that in general the females are smarter than us males.

5. Do you feel personally free of sexual bias?

As I have said, I have not practiced any gender exclusiveness at lectures, discussions, or ceremonies.

7. Can you discern, by her energy, whether or not a woman is menstruating?

I have not thought much about whether a woman was on her moon or not. Occasionally I have noticed irritability and been told why when I asked. Occasionally I have supplied medicine to relieve excessive cramps. Otherwise it is a nothing thing to me.

8. Do you experience cycles that follow moon rhythms?

I know that my male rhythms follow the moon's rhythms as well as other natural cycles. I would think that anyone who is in balance would be part of these rhythms.

9. Would you feel it inappropriate for a woman to direct a Sun Dance, to be a "Road Chief" for peyote ceremonies, or to fill other roles usually restricted by gender?

For myself, if a woman feels moved or guided to conduct or lead a ceremony, has no ulterior motives, and does it with honor, respect, humility, and love, there can be no harm. The same conditions apply to males.

10. Is it beneficial for men and women to ceremonialize together?

I feel that for peace and harmony to prevail we must share in ceremonies, councils, and all activities. There must be openness and truth, no secret activity.

NINA WOLF

1. Have you ever experienced sexual bias that obstructed (or attempted to obstruct) your spiritual work? If so, how did you respond to it?

Yes, mostly from older men of mixed blood and Catholic training. I respond directly, e.g., when accused of usurping the power at Rebirth Gathering: "You have organized the women and taken over the power." Walking Wolf: "I know, Little Brother, the pain in your heart." I call this diplomacy. In general I will avoid such confrontation, withdraw, and ignore such interference with the work at hand. The issue seems to be a capitalistic exploitive notion of power as *power over* instead of *power with*. Power as a commodity with which to exploit others for one's own comfort and acquired material wealth is a mainstream notion in the culture at large. Women as well as men act this notion out, often with other women.

2. What are your beliefs regarding menstrual taboos and women's "moontime"?

I consider moontime as a time of power with the Earth and cleansing for the individual. I have even dedicated a circle to women on their moon. A young pipe carrier just released from prison was doing a memorial pipe for his teacher as part of this circle. He is a traditional Blackfoot. He had a brother of his pass the pipe so that no woman could actually touch it. He left that circle smiling and in much good humor and empowerment; so did the women.

3. Do you conduct gender-exclusive ceremonies? If so, do these make up the bulk of your work?

I do not intentionally conduct gender-exclusive ceremonies. Most of my work is with women. I consider this phenomenon a function of our time.

4. Do you believe there is an inherent difference in men's and women's spiritual natures, practices, and destinies?

No. Contrary to the stance of most formal religions, I do not believe women are inferior in their capacity to achieve spiritual development because of their childbearing function. Rather, I believe that the ability to bear children often makes it easier for women to "hear" the voices of the natural world.

5. Do you feel personally free of sexual bias?

Yes, as much as one can in our culture. I presently look more like my father than any other family member. I have the good fortune to spend most of my life outside of a sexist culture.

6. Do you lead any all-men's sweats or ceremonies?

I have not led any all-men's sweats or ceremonies. I have no negative feelings about being asked to do so.

7. Can you discern, by her energy, whether or not a woman is menstruating?

Yes.

8. Do your menstrual cycles follow moon rhythms?

Yes. Long past menses . . . I lost a child after menopause. Still the physical and psychic changes of menses and ovulation continue with the moon.

9. Would you feel it inappropriate for a woman to direct a Sun Dance, to be a "Road Chief" for peyote ceremonies, or to fill other roles usually restricted by gender?

No. I do not include the Sun Dance among the traditional forms I practice. From my personal history, I cannot at this time participate in any form of physical sacrifice. I already gave at the office. I have road-chiefed for peyote ceremonies (nontraditional).

10. Is it beneficial for men and women to ceremonialize together?

Yes. In hope such custom will be revived among the New Villages. This is how community is maintained in a sacred manner.

LEWIS SAWAQUAT

1. Have you ever experienced sexual bias that obstructed your spiritual work?

No.

2. What are your beliefs regarding menstrual taboos and women's "moontime"?

Same as question #7 about race [see page 39]. However, I respect other's taboos if they are participating in one of "my" ceremonies.

3. Do you conduct gender-exclusive ceremonies? If so, do these make up the bulk of your work?

If requested by participants I will conduct gender-exclusive ceremonies, but I discourage it. I strongly prefer the harmony and balance of "mixed" participation.

4. Do you believe there is an inherent difference in men's and women's spiritual natures, practices, and destinies?

"Below" the level of pure spirit there is duality. One form of this duality is sexuality. Any one human is endowed with a dominant physical sex. It is therefore essential that he or she get in touch with their true spiritual nature.

5. Do you feel personally free of sexual bias?

Consciously yes, but what about cultural and societal norms we are not even conscious of?

6. Do you lead any all-women's sweats or ceremonies?

Yes.

7. Can you discern, by her energy, whether or not a woman is menstruating?

No.

9. Would you feel it inappropriate for a woman to direct a Sun Dance, to be a "Road Chief" for peyote ceremonies, or to fill other roles usually restricted by gender?

No.

10. Is it beneficial for men and women to ceremonialize together?

Absolutely, unless the ceremony is appropriately gender specific as in "full moon" or "warrior" ceremonies.

CHARLA HAWKWIND-HERMANN

1. Have you ever experienced sexual bias that obstructed your spiritual work?

I am very excited about being a woman ceremonialist. I have had more opportunity to participate in and lead Native American ritual than most. I know that when I am "moontime" there is a more appropriate ceremony for me to do and I enjoy the opportunity to be with myself and within myself.

2. What are your beliefs regarding menstrual taboos and women's "moontime"?

As more women learn to love the moontime rituals, it will feel that the men are missing something, not the women. I learned this one year when I was not able to sundance because my moontime came on the first day—after I had prepared for a year, fasted and quested for seven days prior, had made the one thousand prayer ties, etc. I was given a great gift to learn to dance with the moon.

3. Do you conduct gender-exclusive ceremonies? If so, do these make up the bulk of your work?

I lead many women's rituals, but have sat at the sides of dozens of male elders to provide "mixed" rituals. I have poured healing lodges for men only and led a warrior's dance at the side of my elders this summer. My partner and I (Tarwater) lead mixed-lodge and vision quest programs. We each hold a role to balance the other, and are known for our work to assist in the relationship of family—which means all genders and races.

4. Do you believe there is an inherent difference in men's and women's spiritual natures, practices, and destinies?

Yes, women have it all over the men. They keep the recipes and the magics together. I don't know any good medicine man who doesn't have a really wonderful wife who keeps the pieces together as an ongoing part of life.

5. Do you feel personally free of sexual bias?

Yes.

6. Do you lead any all-men's sweats or ceremonies?

Only for special healing work—then it is one-on-one. Gender is not important. We are moving molecules to make a transition.

7. Can you discern, by her energy, whether or not a woman is menstruating?

Yes, her energy spirals counterclockwise down into the Earth. It pulls opposite to how we pour the lodge, moving energy from the base to the crown. Thus, we hold moon lodge to accommodate that process—not in a hot lodge but in a comfortable cabin area.

9. Would you feel it inappropriate for a woman to direct a Sun Dance, to be a "Road Chief" for peyote ceremonies, or to fill other roles usually restricted by gender?

I know several old women who do, quietly, and some of us are being trained for future roles in an Earth Change scenario (ten women to one man—potential population base).

10. Is it beneficial for men and women to ceremonialize together?

Our planet and her people are out of balance. Men and women need to come together to create united healing. I am all for getting together. I am also one who thinks we all have the need to do some gender-specific healing before we can talk in community.

Brooke Medicine Eagle

1. Have you ever experienced sexual bias that obstructed your spiritual work?

Although it is perhaps not what you are asking, I have experienced a lot of sexual harassment from elders and others who wanted me to sleep with them in order for me to be given the teachings. I can't really say how much men have this same experience. Being what I think of as a "mouthy," assertive female who is not stopped or cowed by being in disfavor with the "good old boys" (whether red or white or whatever) has caused me to be unpopular with those groups. I have responded by going more and more directly to Mother Earth and Father Spirit for guidance.

2. What are your beliefs regarding menstrual taboos and women's "moontime"?

I think the old ways have very good basis in ceremonial and good health reasons. In all cases, I find situational flexibility to make good sense. [Included with Brooke's reply are these quotes taken from her book *Buffalo Woman Comes Singing*]:

> The question always comes up about Moon women being asked to leave ceremonies by traditional elders. This has caused many hard feelings, especially when these women don't have knowledge of their natural Moon function at the time, and when the elders do not give them this information. . . . I do not believe that this energy [of menses], which is so connected with life, can cause great harm. That energy is never naturally negative or evil in any way.
>
> There are however, some reasonable explanations for this prac- tice of stepping aside, which I believe were understood by the women who made these rules long ago. Men have followed these rules, and perhaps become rigid with them. Yet *they* can only confuse us when *we* do not know our own bodies and cycles well enough through our own Moon experience. When we know ourselves deeply in this way, no one outside us will have to tell us what to do—we will know within.
>
> These are the reasons experience has shown me. First of all, if we Moon women are using ourselves well, we will be retreating to quest for vision to serve our people.
>
> Secondly, a Moon woman's body is already doing a deep cleans- ing; she is low on energy and is called to rest and quiet for reasons of her own health. The stress and energy of interaction or focused ceremony does not serve her, especially the intense stress of a hot sweat lodge. It is not only unnecessary but contra-indicated.
>
> Thirdly, the function of the Moon time is to be quiet, to go within, to release outward things, to move through structure into more subtle levels of being. Thus, this very feminine energy could be termed de-structuring. It is not about form, it is not about

rigidly set ways, it is not about anything involving time and order, it is not about anything linear. A ritual or ceremony, however, often has a set procedure and an outcome that it is meant to produce in a certain amount of time. If a Moon woman comes into that setting, her very powerful energy is moving to de-structure everything it touches, and thus she has a disturbing effect on the outcome.

All these things suggest to me that Moon women are better occupied in other ways.

3. Do you conduct gender-exclusive ceremonies? If so, do these make up the bulk of your work?

I conduct moon (menstrual) ceremonies specifically for women; all other ceremonies I can think of are open. I do conduct many workshops for women because I have been given certain information specific to women. Had I been given the same kind and amount of information for men, I would certainly be spending the same kind of time with them. I do think it useful for the genders to spend time separate from each other, learning about themselves, only so that they can come back together in a better way for the good of all things. It is never about being better or worse, right or wrong. We are all the children of Great Spirit, and were put on this good earth to learn to live well together in the many forms available.

4. Do you believe there is an inherent difference in men's and women's spiritual natures, practices, and destinies?

Yes, I do. All my teachers speak of not only physiological but spiritual and emotional differences that lead to different practices and rituals in the gender-specific groups.

5. Do you feel personally free of sexual bias?

I certainly hope so. I believe I see the challenges and beauties of both sexes, and wish for us to work in ways to heal each other and all things. I do not believe any one group or sex has the great key, although women are being called to the front spiritually and ecologically right now to teach and portray the nurturing and renewing of life energy that is their birthright and is so vital right now.

7. Can you discern, by her energy, whether or not a woman is menstruating?

At this time, I cannot, but I know it profoundly affects the energy around her.

8. Do your menstrual cycles follow moon rhythms?

Most often my moon cycle follows moon rhythms. However, when I am traveling internationally and working with large groups it is likely to be thrown off and take some time to recover.

9. Would you feel it inappropriate for a woman to direct a Sun Dance, to be a "Road Chief" for peyote ceremonies, or to fill other roles usually restricted by gender?

I feel that in most cases, if there is a woman who wants to lead what are normally gender-restricted ceremonies and the elders find her qualified, she should certainly be allowed. I think in the old days among Native people this was more usual, because each individual case was better understood in a small tribal group. Today, the "cowboy/Indian macho," which comes from the dominant culture, has very strongly influenced Native culture. And in general, the feminine/Goddess ways have been put down.

10. Is it beneficial for men and women to ceremonialize together?

You bet! It is vital and necessary for the balance and holding of the full circle of life in a good way.

AXIS

1. Have you ever experienced sexual bias that obstructed your spiritual work?

No, but I tend not to go places where I won't be allowed to be who I am. I've been to plenty of places that really pissed me off though (being offended).

2. What are your beliefs regarding menstrual taboos and women's "moontime"?

I believe! (Hallelujah!) that most women of certain age groups menstruate. That it is connected to the reproductive function, which makes it sacred. That there is a subtle freeing of energy from belief that occurs. That it is an opportunity, not a curse. [Included here, to expand on this, is an article Axis wrote that appeared in the 1992 Samhain Yule issue of *Notes from Taychopera* as a response to an article that dealt with menstrual beliefs in very negative and absolute terms. With Axis's permission I quote some of his reply.]

The moontime is the break-up of the matrix of the lunar cycle of the human female womb. When any matrix is broken the energy that used to flow in certain patterns toward specific ends is momentarily freed. This energy is free energy, not evil energy, not good energy, just capable of becoming anything. All free energy is a source of power for a magician, medicine person, or individual so inclined (of either sex). It can be used to help and heal and also, as the [article's] author dwells upon, to harm and hurt. Regardless, there is no movement of medicine, no creative magick, without free energy being available in one form or another. It seems true to me that free energy, being unbound from belief, is the manifestation of creative power. Without free energy there is no growing or moving or change. Free energy is part of the power of nature, and its presence in the human psycho-spiritual make-up is a gift of the Mystery.

There is a tremendous karmic shift which follows the purely human shift from estrus cycle to menstrual cycle in the human female which affects both male and female sexuality. This shift is the gift of the sacred fire. This gift is nearly always appropriated by male-oriented religious forms and symbols as well as separated and concealed from its feminine source.

Nearly all religions teach us fear and separation from our gift of creativity. We are taught to fear our gift and birthright. It is not a question of whether the gift is used or not for it is always used. Either in light or in darkness the creative fire manifests. Look around you at the world and you will see the tremendous harm done when the sacred fire is distorted and feared. Things are still created but they are done wrongly and without balance.

The relation of the creative power to the people is not one of master to slave (doctrines of separation) but of root to flower. Is it the freedom of energy that emanates from the moontime woman that is really what is so frightening? It is true to me (an opinion about an observation) that free energies need to be handled properly to produce specific magickal effects or to become vehicles of the sacred. So it is important that a sacred matrix is created or invoked that allows free energy to be directed in a manner that helps and heals. It is apparent to me that the creation or invocation of sacred matrices for moontime spirituality is not rightly done with the exclusion of the feminine source of life.

However, these free energies do not emanate exclusively from moontime woman. Energies are freed from belief with every orgasm and every meal. With every disillusionment and disappointment. With every great sacrifice we make. Any time one thing ends and before another begins.

I speak (or write) and am unafraid to do so. I still pray every sunrise for the awakening to come, for people and all beings of all the nations to live together in good ways. For there to be peace, respect, recognition, understanding, and love between all human beings, and I long for the time to come when the sacred dream that unfolds from the medicine wheel to someday become flesh.

3. Do you conduct gender-exclusive ceremonies?

No, and I generally don't even like to go to them.

4. Do you believe there is an inherent difference in men's and women's spiritual natures, practices, and destinies?

I believe! (the cry of the damned) that the sexuality of our bodies and our relationships to it is a powerful force in our wholeness of being and therefore is a factor in our spiritual nature. Beyond this, there is no definitive or constrictive nature to gender, per se, that is inherent.

5. Do you feel personally free of sexual bias?

I like to make love to women and not to men. Is that a bias? Other than that I would think no. Except (thinking deeper) that I raised my sons to never hit women and I did not say that about men, nor have I ever said it to my daughter. Perhaps I am minimally and subliminally biased.

6. Do you lead any all-women's sweats or ceremonies?

No.

7. Can you discern, by her energy, whether or not a woman is menstruating?

No, I check the wastepaper basket in the bathroom, then act like I'm psychically gifted.

9. Would you feel it inappropriate for a woman to direct a Sun Dance, to be a "Road Chief" for peyote ceremonies, or to fill other roles usually restricted by gender?

I don't know, never having been to any of these. Do you need a phallus for them?

10. Is it beneficial for men and women to ceremonialize together?

Yes.

SANDRA INGERMAN

What I teach people is how to connect with helping spirits, and I don't see that the helping spirits have a different way of looking at men's and women's spirituality. I advise women to be very aware of their own energy at the time of menstruation, to watch for themselves whether they feel they want to be more inward and not working on people or whether they feel they have a lot of power available to them at that time and they actually want to channel that into healing energy. Only the woman herself is going to know where her own personal energy is at during that time.

MEDICINE HAWK WILBURN

1. Have you ever experienced sexual bias that obstructed your spiritual work?

Yes. Many women's groups are populated by individuals who have gone far overboard in a crusade to make all men pay for the way some men have treated women in the past (and present). I have often been the brunt of their animosity in both personal and teaching situations. I didn't do anything to these women. I can't do anything about what men have done to them. I ain't no carpenter's son. It's hard enough just being an Indian.

2. What are your beliefs regarding menstrual taboos and women's "moontime"?

There's no reason for it. All those taboos about menstruation are rooted in male insecurity. A lot has been said about women's power during moontime being "too much for men to deal with." Get real! I've even heard it said that bears would attack sweat lodges containing menstruating women. This all *sounds* spiritual, but since I don't write for the tabloids I don't pay any attention to it. I've taken a lot of flak because many traditionalists are not ready to let go of this taboo. They resent me because I am free from it. You know, men menstruate too, although not with the same physical phenomena. During menstruation women have been accused of erratic behavior. When men have a similar "sun cycle" they do similar things: get drunk, get in fights, speed in their cars, and do things that involve great physical risk. Not all men, of course, and not all the time, but they experience a similar "cleansing" time and respond in kind.

3. Do you conduct gender-exclusive ceremonies? If so, do these make up the bulk of your work?

Yes, we have "men's mysteries" meetings. Parts of the meetings are open to women. I don't think there's anything in these meetings women don't already know. I think the whole idea is just to get away from women and be with men sometimes. If the women really wanted to, we'd let them come to any of these get-togethers. They are not the bulk of my work.

4. Do you believe there is an inherent difference in men's and women's spiritual natures, practices, and destinies?

No, otherwise there would be no homosexuality.

5. Do you feel personally free of sexual bias?

No, I was abducted by the Southern Baptist Church at an early age, kept captive for eighteen years, and then released into Vietnam. I learned a little bias from the church (scripturally supported) and added a little of my own resentment against women, because of what only a few women had done to me. Even though those women had done bad things to me, they did them because they were jerks, not because they were women. I took it all personally, however, and projected my own bigotry onto all women—which proves I am a shallow and resentful person. I'm in a huge crowd.

7. *Can you discern, by her energy, whether or not a woman is menstruating?*

The one I live with, definitely. Others, no. I think it's individual.

9. *Would you feel it inappropriate for a woman to direct a Sun Dance, to be a "Road Chief" for peyote ceremonies, or to fill other roles usually restricted by gender?*

Definitely not. Such things were never gender specific in my tribe.

10. *Is it beneficial for men and women to ceremonialize together?*

Yes, the main ceremonies should be like real life.

6

LOOKING WITHIN:
CONTEMPLATIONS ON GENDER

SELF-IMAGE

Focus your attention on your gender. Name the qualities you associate with your sex and investigate the implications of these qualities. Explore the physical, emotional, mental, and spiritual levels of manifestation as you identify the qualities.

Now imagine yourself to be the other gender.

What physical, emotional, mental, and spiritual qualities do you
 link with this gender?
Do you experience any or all of them in relation to your usual
 self?
Instead of a polarity, can you see all the qualities as a spectrum or
 range of possibilities having no gender label?
Are you comfortable with this?
Is it useful?

What do you see as the differences in experience between the
genders?

What feelings of envy, fear, attraction, ease, and so on, do you
have toward being one or the other sex?

How would your spiritual path or experience change if your
gender changed?

Are there ever times when you don't think of yourself as being a
man or a woman?

Are there ever times when gender is not a primary awareness
within social interactions?

What do you like most and least about being a man or a woman?

Do you see these things as biologically ordained or as
conditioning?

IDENTIFYING STEREOTYPES

Mentally inventory the occupations or roles people fill in this world.
Are there any (besides childbearing) that you see as inherently gender
exclusive?

As you consider this, suspend your conditioned assumptions as best
you can, remembering the range of different sorts of men and women
there are in the world. As you imagine men in stereotypically female
roles or women in what are usually male occupations take note of
your emotional reactions to these ideas.

What is it in the past that has determined gender exclusivity in
society's roles?

What patterns of relationship and culture do these conditionings
reveal?

What is revealed by current trends?

What are you doing personally to perpetuate or to alter these
patterns?

When you interact with children, what gender messages do you
convey through your words, acts, and community role?

Do your messages encourage freedom of self-expression?

Some areas to examine:

- Differences in toys or activities you offer to children of each gender
- Differences in your level of comfort with children of each gender
- Differences in the kind of information you offer
- Differences in your response to achievement, inquiry, rambunctiousness, challenge to authority, illness or injury, crying, hitting, interruption, physical contact, appeals for affection, and so on
- Differences in the advice or help you give to children of each gender
- Differences in your expectations of children of each gender

As you examine these differences, ask yourself the following questions:

How conditioned are your attitudes and responses?
How do they reflect or differ from the way you were raised?
What would a world of sexual equality look like to you?
Would you be happy in such a world?

THE LANGUAGE OF DUALITY

View the universe as a dual cosmos having male and female polarities of expression. Divide a paper in half, longways, with one side for male and the other for female. Put each of the following aspects of the natural world in one column or the other according to your own perspectives: Earth, Sky, Ocean, Thunder, Lightning, Fog, Rain, Oak tree, Willow tree, Clouds, Quartz crystals, Sweetgrass, Sage, Cedar, Tobacco, Obsidian, Butterfly, Eagle, Hurricane, Tornado, Rainbow, Volcano, Sun, Moon.
Look over your lists.

Was the list making a difficult process?
Are the columns equal in length?
What patterns emerge from your groupings?
What do these patterns reveal about your perspectives?

Now take each thing on the list and switch its positioning. For example, if you put Earth in the female column, switch it over to the male column. Can you genuinely shift perspective in this way? Is it difficult? Is it helpful?

Consider the kinship terms of Grandmother, Grandfather, Father, Mother, Sister, Brother, Uncle, Aunt. What emotions do you associate with each? What are their connotations?

Instead of the male/female categories, designate kinship terms for the things on the list. Does this change your relationship to them? How?

Play with this, shifting the terms around to see how you react to different combinations.

Now remove all the categories. Remove them mentally as well.

Can you do this completely?

Is it difficult?

Can you still have a relationship with these things without a
     kinship or sexual designation?

How does this change things?

Would working this way (without duality) in the long term
     change how you view yourself?

WHO ASSIGNED YOU THIS ROLE?

Visualize yourself as a disembodied consciousness. You draw to yourself a context for the unfolding of experience. An aspect of this context is a human body.

Imagine you are a baby. Consciousness opens to context. Words are spoken to you, a habitat surrounds you, relationships evolve. You receive input from senses, from subtle levels of receptivity, from memory. You receive instruction about your identity. You grow.

Beliefs, opinions, judgments, and attitudes are formed, and you identify with them as instructed. You are a he or a she, a him or a her. Definition is received, parameters described deliberately or thoughtlessly. You assimilate these teachings and identify with them. You pass them on to others.

List ten words to describe yourself.

Are they adjectives?

Nouns?

Are they physical characteristics?

Personality traits?

Roles you enact?

Are they gender related?

Do you think other people would describe you the same way? (If you don't know, ask people.)

Who taught you to see yourself in these terms?

Where did these perceptions come from?

When did you start seeing yourself this way?

Are you happy with these self-perceptions?

How important—what use—are these attributes to you?

What is your path of freedom?

INFLUENCES

Be very conscious of the present moment and of your state of being within it. Check in with what is going on in your body, your thoughts, and your emotions. Make no attempt to change anything, just be aware.

Extend that awareness into your environment. What factors are influencing your body, thoughts, and emotions? Weather? Moon phase? Activity? Locality? Posture? Hunger? Digestion? Lack of sleep? Season? Drugs or energy modifiers? Proximity to others? Noise? Music? Aromas? Pain? Astrological configurations? Time of day? Type of lighting that is present? The clothes you are wearing? Leftover energies from events or personal interactions? Other things?

Consider these influences and their degrees of effect on your present state of being.

How many things are you conscious of in daily life?

During ceremonial occasions?

Which ones do you consider particularly influential?

Do you consciously try to integrate, modify, or make use of these influences?

What do you do to establish or maintain harmony with your environment?

How aware are you (usually) of your state of being?

How much responsibility do you take for regulating your energy
in relation to your environment?

In relation to yourself?

In relation to others?

THE WOMB LODGE

Consider closely what you know about menstruation. If you are a woman, also recall your particular experiences with your cycle.

How would you characterize the energies?

How do they seem to affect you?

Those around you?

What are your feelings about menstrual blood?

What effect do you feel these energies have on ceremony?

Consider other energies sometimes present at ceremonies.

Are any of them comparable to menstruation?

What is the purpose of making something taboo?

Are there other approaches to communal dynamics or to natural
energies that would serve the people as well or better?

What role does fear play in the enforcing of taboos?

What role does belief play?

If a taboo is not universal, does it affect only those who believe
in it?

Visualize the womb as a sacred lodge. A mysterious place that, like the sweat lodge, can enlarge itself to contain whatever needs to be there—a place where the worlds meet and where life's embodiment can come into manifestation. A place where dreams are nourished and evolved.

Visualize the lodge of the womb, understanding that it is not separate from the web of energies that is a woman's wholeness, or from the larger web that is the cosmos. It functions within a context, a matrix. Hormonal energies shift their balances as the cycle moves. The womb lodge gradually creates accommodations suitable for receiving and nuturing the egg that may become a baby. At ovulation the hormonal energies sing of sexual urges, union, and fulfillment. The lodge is prepared for welcome.

If no conception occurs, the cycle continues in its usual pattern. Hormones shift at menstruation to cause the release of the rich lining built up for reception of a fertilized egg. The lodge sends out what was not to be used this time. For a woman hoping for pregnancy this may bring sadness. For a woman whose contraception failed this may bring great relief. For a woman experiencing pain or imbalance her period may invoke irritability. For a woman whose menstrual cycle is not a focus of attention the bleeding time may be a minor shift in energies relative to other aspects of life.

What flows from the womb during menstruation is not unclean. The womb is not moving from impurity to purity as it bleeds. It is not clearing away something harmful any more than when it releases a placenta after a child is born. The moon has a natural cycle of change, the seasons likewise, and so do human bodies. As you visualize the womb lodge, honor its keeper and her potential to move in a sacred way with all her energies.

SEXUALITY IN SPIRITUAL WORK

In all embodied life is the desire to be and to become. The primal fire of sexuality is part of creation's alchemy. Sexuality urges union in service to renewal. It calls to life and is life's dance. Sexuality: attraction, movement, heat, energy, an aspect of creative power, an ecstasy within relationship. Contemplate the way this energy is used—consciously or unconsciously—in ceremonial or spiritual work. See it in relation to dance, to drumming, to the combining of elements, to alignment with various forces, to acts of merging, yielding, union, and creative transcendence.

How does the realization of this energy's presence in spiritual work change your perspective of spirituality? Of sexuality?

Consider the abuse of sexuality in spiritual settings, or the fear of sexuality, or the confusion about it. What ways can you think of to heal this? What changes in ceremonial form or in attitudes and behaviors would restore clarity to our interactions with sexuality?

PART THREE

COMMUNITY

7

REFLECTIONS ON COMMUNITY

There are three levels of community that relate to this book's topics. The first is the "shamanic community," which I think of as the people who provide services derived from shamanic spirituality, whether Native or native, traditional or contemporary. This community is far-flung and diverse, but often as full of gossip and intrigue as a small town. The second community level is that of each practitioner's immediate surroundings—the local network—and the third level is the larger matrix of "all my relations": the community of life.

In the first level, the shamanic community, move the teachers, healers, ceremonialists, medicine people, shamans, and counselors—Native, non-Native, and métis. An anthropologist would cringe at my conflating these categories under the heading of shamanism, but this is meant to be not an academic definition but just a generalized working term. This is a community, not of proximity or even of shared understandings, but of shamanistic service.

A medicine man visiting my area came to my home to ask permission before conducting a ceremony in my local area. His request revealed his wisdom in all three levels of community, as well as his recognition of traditional courtesy. It reflected his awareness of local spirit activity, local community politics, and the interrelationship between shamans. The beneficial mixing of these networks of energy is a subtle and important art. When medicine people visited our area and led sweats or conducted ceremonies, they were usually mindful of their influence on the seen and unseen levels of local habitat and community, spiritual and temporal. When this awareness is not present or not acted upon in responsible ways, there can be a disruption of balances, the consequences of which are quite tangible.

Many teachers do a great deal of traveling, offering seminars, appearing at gatherings, leading pilgrimages, and conducting ceremonies. More than ever, teachers are on the move; their personal communities of students and associates are spread far and wide over the globe. This means that the practitioners come into each other's spheres of influence frequently and have much occasion to affect those spheres through their work and through how they relate to other practitioners.

Dances of ego among practitioners are nothing new. Entertaining and revealing as these often are, a destructive element of mean-spiritedness often lies beneath caustic observations and innuendo. Gossip as a form of peer review performs a useful function until it enters the realm where words become poison instead of antidote. Criticism may arise from and serve connectedness—mutual effort and excellence—or it may distance and compete for ascendancy.

It is frustrating to hear pettiness endlessly bandied about, then note how the ranks close in collective denial about vital issues such as racism or sexual misconduct. In Canada some reservation women finally appealed to outside authorities for relief from epidemic sexual violence and incest. Their tribal elders were doing nothing to remedy the situation because some of them were themselves the abusers. The women, in desperation, went against custom and sensibilities by calling for outside help. To be silent or to squabble when mature communication is needed is to succumb to a loss of perspective.

How can the shamanic community serve the well-being of others if practitioners become too caught up in their positions in the elite hierarchy to attend to their work? How can practitioners develop and learn if they are preoccupied with trying to appear infallible? One misstep and enemies close in. Relax your guard and be blindsided.

Practitioners become more engaged with performance than with conducting medicine; they worry about their allies on the workshop circuit instead of looking to spirit alliances. Money becomes a big issue. Shamans become celebrities instead of mediators. Shortcuts tempt the beleaguered, and ethics take a beating. This is not the whole picture, of course, but it is an accurate sketch of one part of it.

Beside the backbiting between practitioners is the targeting of teachers by separatist groups and organizations. Teachers in the public eye make easy targets, but much of the protest against them is based on gossip, assumption, and relentless prejudice, not on direct knowledge of or interaction with the teachers in question. Communication and understanding do not seem to be the goals of these protests, so what results is a further fueling of anger and divisiveness, not a resolution of issues and ills on either side. The war goes on, with oppression lending its deadening weight to which ever side invokes it through aggression, lies, fear, and dominance. Sometimes we learn the wrong things from each other.

Teachers caught up in commercialization, confused teaching, egotism, or exploitation will reap the natural consequences of these. What is needed is honest, healthy feedback, not hounding by the envious or the hateful.

Teachers oversensitized to criticism have difficulty distinguishing good advice or soundly differing perspectives from jealous remarks and unproductive put-downs. The proliferation of bickering has made useful criticism hard to offer or receive. Teachers end up having followers instead of a natural, accessible place in community.

I remember all the bustling around people did in preparation for the arrival of the Native camp chief at the Canadian gathering. His lodge was set up and made comfortable, food concerns were dealt with, escorts were briefed. He was treated royally, his needs responded to devotedly. This was a lovely demonstration of caring and respect, but it was certainly not traditional. In the old days, camp chief was a role that required much giving and keen awareness of the needs of others. The old-time camp chiefs made sure everyone else was taken care of before seeing to their own situations. I don't begrudge our camp chief his fine reception; I speak of it as an example of how community dynamics have changed.

The context in which the shaman now operates little resembles—even on reservations—the community of the past, yet the shaman's role is still that of healer and mediator. Do our new versions of community see that role in a mutually useful way? Does the shamanic community help the individual practitioner to mesh harmoniously in local community? Is the shamanic community so self-absorbed that it is only relevant to itself?

There was an Iroquois ceremonialist in the area where I was living. He sent his wife to attend one of our sweat lodges, apparently to check us out. Some time later a friend who participated in the lodges was visiting this man and his wife and found herself being brow-beaten over the way the lodges were conducted. Oddly enough, his complaint was not about taboo violation or other predictable contentions but about the attendee's prayers. He claimed that people should pray only to "Grandfather" and not be praying about things of the Earth or about personal concerns. He announced that he was going to come over and tear our lodge down.

When I heard this I was astonished. I wrote the man a letter saying that if he had problems about how our ceremonies were conducted, he should make his complaints directly to me and not bully innocent guests in his home. The man neither replied to my letter nor appeared at our lodge.

There are productive ways of dealing with one another about differences. Sometimes a misunderstanding seems almost deliberate—it is easier to write each other off than to make efforts to reach tolerance, if not agreement. If we do not make the effort, we become poor examples of healers. We become more and more locked into our individual positions. Elitism, shamanic one-upmanship, racial and gender issues, factionalism, pride, argument over spiritual technicalities, and lack of trust or openness are banes of the shamanic community. Positive elements include stimulus for growth, reduction of the characteristic healer's isolation, and—perhaps most precious—a sense of spirit's pervasive flow. For shamanism and the shamanic community to flourish, these positive elements need to emerge, not just coincidentally, but through active nurturance. As with race and gender, whatever our differences, the core of commitment to healing should preempt all lesser alignments.

The second aspect of community is that of the practitioner's local area of service. I use the term *local* loosely to include people connected through the mail or in regular contact with a particular teacher or healer. This is the practitioner's personal precinct of relationship and influence.

Traditionally this was literally a community or tribal group. These days, many shamans are "at large" practitioners, traveling, writing books, or giving teachings to visiting seekers rather than working amid a settlement. There are distinctions between these two forms of involvement and, among some traditionals, a discounting of medicine people who don't have a locality of practice.

This bias is based not only on custom but also on the particulars of what community practice encompassses. Long-term involvement with one group of people—families who probably knew your forebears and will be neighbors to your children—requires long-term evidence of competence and integrity. There's no escape from reputation, good or bad, in community practice. People watch and remember, lineages are known, exaggerated claims are unmasked. The shaman's role, when part of a local community, bears a continuity and partakes in a cultural and environmental context. This context gives foundation and orientation to the work enacted.

This situation is not duplicated in a practice that serves clients instead of neighbors, or instructs students without long-term follow-up. When distances are great, it is more difficult to ascertain results and accountability. Money becomes the primary medium of relationship, and participation in a social or cultural network of balances is lacking. These lacks have significant impact on the work itself and on the overall evolution of shamanic practice. They create a different pattern of relationship both between shaman and society and between shaman and power.

The popularity of what Michael Harner calls "core shamanism" grows steadily in a society whose mainstream is a polyglot of transplanted cultures. With hypnotherapists, Jungian counselors, and New Age enthusiasts all hanging out their shamanic shingles, what does being a shaman really mean anymore in terms of community? Where are the traditional links between shaman and society? Where is the reality of shamanic experience in relation to modern practitioners and their practice? Orphaned from cultural belief shamanic technique becomes separate from natural interrelationships that demand the practitioner be in touch with the ecologies of community and environment. More and more it is personal growth that is the shamanic precinct, and the work becomes more oriented to individual psychology than to sacred mystery or the realization of a larger wholeness. Great loss may be suffered if core shamanism entirely eclipses cultural shamanism or doesn't evolve into a new cultural shamanism.

It is important that shamanism be allied with community on a level where the work is part of an ongoing, neighborly interplay of concerned sharing, engagement, and respect. This kind of alliance also makes the shaman less of a celebrity, consequently making it easier for practitioners to avoid the pitfalls of psychological isolation.

Of all community issues, probably the most hotly discussed is that of money. Money, these days, is usually the vehicle of interaction between urban shaman and community. In times past, tribal societies had a broader sense of community dynamics; the spiritual specialist's role was considered just as integral—and in need of material support—as any other's in the tribe.

These days, medicine is often treated more as a commodity than a service. Shamans are now outsiders to mainstream society. There is no consensus of belief. Deep schisms appear between Native and non-Native, purist and eclectic, and core and cultural shamanists, as well as between shamanism and mainstream religions and medical systems. As a result, practitioners tend to engage with individuals instead of community and to use the medium of money rather than a network of communal balances.

When Natives talk about not wanting to sell their spirituality, I think they are objecting not to material support of teachers and medicine people, or to exchanges being made for services, but to the assumption that Native spirituality, which weaves the fabric of Native identity can be bought. Respectful interest that honors and supports is not the same as acquisitive demand that intrudes and grasps.

Native Americans derive the least material benefit, of anyone, from the popularization of shamanism. The big money flows into commercial, non-Native pockets, thus exacerbating racial division. The solution is not necessarily to redirect the cash flow but to reconsider what is being propagated.

Money is a mirror of values. What is being valued in the way money is used in relation to spirituality? When shamans charge hefty fees for giving teachings or doing shamanic work, they convey the message that they must be offering something very valuable. If a medicine person gives away healing and counsel or simply accepts whatever is offered in return, that person's work is often not valued. Part of the problem is the fragmentation of true community. Another part is modern attitudes about worth.

Without a price tag, how does a person know what to give for spiritual services? In our society we're used to price tags and market values. We're not used to attuning to what is needed to nourish balance in a web of well-being. It takes greater consideration and vulnerability to discern those true needs and balances than to simply pay the listed fee. Paying the fee is an act of responsibility, but it doesn't carry the same power of participation that acting upon right balances does, and it puts a perhaps inappropriate burden on the practitioner to define value for someone else. It may also affect how the medicine itself operates.

Many people are uncomfortable with having spirituality and money in the same realm at all. There are total purists, total capitalists, and everything in between. Some people say it's OK to charge for teachings but not ceremonies, or drums but not pipes, or cassette tapes but not drums, and so on. Each choice reveals where lines are drawn between the sacred and the mundane or the not-so-sacred. Leaving out the issue of bald exploitation—which is a matter of perspective— why are these lines drawn and when did they historically appear?

The gap between the sacred and the mundane has grown wider and wider throughout the history of many modern cultures and religions. Money has become the monstrous idol we're simultaneously proud and ashamed of worshiping. In order to reconcile spirit to the compromises associated with commerce, we tend to keep money behind the scenes when involved with sacred matters.

But such discretion does not heal our troubled perspectives or give spirituality (or spiritual specialists) rightful recognition within the community. It is the separation of spirit and matter that has made the situation unhealthy, not the presence of money on the altar. If spirituality is seen—and lived—as the vital essence in everything we do, then spirituality can be valued on all levels without shame or predicament. It should not be a realm apart; neither should it be a commodity in service to greed and egotism. There is a natural place for the spiritual specialist in society that will be found when spirituality is implicit in all aspects of daily life.

The third level of community is the web of life, and it is of this that the shaman must be most aware: the known and the unknown, the seen and unseen, the sacred universe. Each practitioner finds his or her own path amid this mandala, and his or her own way of serving the Mystery.

A participant in Crow Sun Dances lived in our area for a time and attended some of our ceremonies until moving to another community. He had differences with how we did things in regard to gender protocols and so on, but attended nonetheless. After he moved away I got word that he spoke of how much he missed our lodges. The ones he currently participated in were conducted in a manner he was more comfortable with, but he said he missed the strength of love he had felt in our ceremonies.

It was good to hear that, because traditions and "ways" change and evolve in their own time. Doing something right doesn't always equal doing something well. Love is a wellness that honors transcendent good. In talking about love I don't mean a warm fuzziness of group bonding or a momentary high feeling, but a power of healing and reconnection to Spirit.

Some members of our community attended a sweat led by a Nootka medicine man. We had never met him. We attended as part of our participation in a joint Native/non-Native response to salmon endangerment due to dams in our region.

It was the strangest sweat I'd ever attended. The shaman seemed malevolent. In the lodge I sat next to a joyful young man whose birthday it happened to be. At one point in the ceremony he asked if he could drink, and the shaman wordlessly tilted the water bucket toward him. The young man cupped water in his hands and drank, splashing some on his face. The shaman then intoned in a solemn voice that the water in the bucket was "tainted" by all our problems and impurities and that the young man was now "doomed for life" by having drunk it. There was consternation and disbelief in the lodge as participants silently struggled to reconcile the shaman's words with his actions in offering the water. The man beside me covered his face and wept, all joy and innocence drained from him. It is still a grievous memory to me, years later.

Following the ceremony several people who attended the sweat came to me with requests for a healing lodge to cleanse themselves of the feelings they carried from that ceremony. I don't know what became of the young man—he was not from our area—but we made prayers for him.

Whatever blunders or entrapments people fall into during ceremony, and whatever the tradition or protocols, no one should ever be told they are doomed for life. The shaman's role is to heal, to teach, to bridge the realms, not to sit in judgment. The shining thread that illumines and enlivens the sacred web is love.

If truth depended on knowing which direction is the correct one for the lodge to face, or whether sage clears away or invokes energies, or if peyote is necessary for transformation, we'd be in big trouble, because every medicine person has his or her own beliefs to offer. Even if a large number of respected specialists concur on a particular vision of truth, time might bring change to that perspective, or the vision might be applicable only to like-minded others. There is a place, distinct from ignorance or scorn, where belief and tradition may be questioned and fresh insight or guidance opened to.

Where would we be without the heyoka's mirror, without the youth's challenge, without the visionary's revelation, without the elder's independence or the renegade's audacity? The council needs many voices and the community much opportunity for caring to manifest and all to be treated as sacred beings. It is not tradition that will sustain and nurture people if beliefs and practices don't carry in their core a living power of love. A form without heart and breath is not alive and will not inspire or heal. Native people have long understood this. I appeal to the adopter of Native medicine ways not to mistake tradition for spirituality itself.

I live on a mountain—rock, clay, sand, trees, animals, cold-flowing springs. The climate is dry, the human community low-income and rural. In living here, in building a home and participating in the web of life, I have to inquire daily, What is the path of harmony here, in this moment? What I do, how I move on the land among my relations, must reflect right kinship here and now. It must be sensitive to the particularities within this daily dance, to what abides here and to how I touch it. Decisions can be instinctive but not arbitrary, and consideration must extend in all directions.

Community is the teacher. It stands in the North on the medicine wheel, the realm of wisdom. It is the mirror, the feedback, the context of realization. To eat, to cut firewood, to own a car, to overturn a stone is to participate in community, consciously or not. We are rearranging the universe. There is no standing apart even in death. Interconnection is the condition of this universe. Nothing is exempt.

Connection is the shaman's specialty, our gift, our work: mediation and sacred relationship. In community we learn to live this. When sitting in council once, I said, "It is easy for me to remember myself as Eagle, as Panther, but much harder to remember myself as Human Being." Sometimes our own kind, who reflect our weaknesses and shadows so challengingly, are the hardest embodiments to be in good relationship with. They reflect hidden struggles and misalignments within our conditioned patterns. The shaman who has faced these mirrors with acceptance, or faced self and seen the eyes of all others, knows an aspect of connectedness that serves both wisdom and compassion.

Always in motion yet never in isolation, life unfolds through pattern and form: the blossoming rose, the leaping deer, the mist rising up the mountainside from the river. The child murmurs in sleep; grasses bend under the wind's sweep. The child breathes, and moonlight pours over quiet rocks. The child grows, climbs the hills of childhood, youth, parenthood, old age. The child becomes ancestor, and winds stroke the grasses where bones turn to soil.

All is endless transformation; being in motion. We miss so much when we become complacent or narrowminded. Shamans who would walk the unseen realms or navigate nonordinary reality should not shy from opening the mind, opening the heart, expanding vision and possibility, embracing transformation. The keepers of the way should also be learners of all that can be known—the first to listen, the last to turn away. It is the mystery, not spiritual career, that is the focus. It is wholeness, not separation, that we believe.

Many of the small stories in this book, of necessity, illustrate conflict or difficulty disproportionate to the bulk of my experience with the Red Road, which has been greatly positive and blessed. I have been fortunate in my interactions and grateful for extraordinary tolerance and kindness encountered on the path. My memories touch on many shared campfires and communal meals, on moments of wry humor and of silent poignancy, and on medicine work that crossed boundaries of race, personality, and currents of time to reach a transcendent mutuality of loving, powerful purpose.

I pray that the words in this book serve well-being and only well-being in all realms, among all people, and I give thanks here to all my teachers—all my relations in Spirit.

I remember a particular honoring ceremony. The people were clustered in a circle with the big drum, listening and watching as various individuals were honored for their work. A pipe was given, and blankets, and then the drum called the honored ones to a slow circuit within the gathered circle.

As the drum sounded and the singing began to rise into the evening sky, more and more people joined the inner circle of dancers. Gradually everyone began moving slowly, with dignity, a turning wheel. Hundreds of feet gently marked the drum's beat upon the grass. Hundreds of feet moved in harmony, respectfully; booted, sandaled, moccasined, sneakered, bare. Feet of children, of elders, of mothers, of youths, of fathers, of all races moved slowly together, in a good way together on the sacred ground.

The singing swelled and stirred the leaves, and touched the sunset, the faces alight with life's beauty. The drum beat within all hearts in that circle that was a river, an honoring that included all.

8

PASSING THE TALKING STICK

GREY WOLF

1. What is the focus of your teaching, healing, or ceremonial work?

The name that I am called, Grey Wolf, signifies "one who leads the people back into conscious awareness of the Oneness of All." If I practice any healing, it is of a spiritual nature. Ceremonies and rituals are tools that I use to establish guideposts along the spiritual path.

2. What direction do you see the shamanic community heading toward?

At the present time I see the shamanic community riding madly off in all directions at the same time.

3. How do you see the dance between tradition and visionary change?

The dance is a very slow one in that today's visionaries will be thought of as traditionals in generations to come.

4. What do you feel are the outstanding ethical abuses, if any, going on in the shamanic community?

It seems to me that the outstanding ethical abuse within the shamanic community is by those who say, "I can do such and such," forgetting that without the Creator they can do nothing.

5. What are your thoughts about money's role in teaching, ceremonial work, and shamanic service?

We have come to accept money as a form having value. I do not know what you need or would like to have, so I can give you an honor gift of money and you can make your own selection. Maybe you do not need sweetgrass, sage, tobacco, or furs. On the other hand, I do not agree with the idea that I will not share these teachings with you unless you give me a fixed number of green frog skins.

6. Do you consider yourself a traditionalist?

I do not consider myself to be a traditionalist. I have been called an iconoclast.

7. What do you feel makes a medicine person a medicine person?

A medicine person? A label placed by others on someone they honor and respect. A deep question that I will think about.

8. How do you feel about the integration of shamanic techniques such as soul retrieval with urban psychological therapy?

Psycho-logical. Psyche, the Spirit or Soul, being of ethereal realms and not bound by material physics, has nothing logical about it. It is not bound by time, space, form, or mass. I can fly in the air, live under water, pass through solid walls or rock, zoom into space, move back and forth through the dimension called time, change my size and form, and be several places at once when I enter the psychic realms. "Psychological" is an oxymoron. I play with words.

9. Do you think closeness with nature is an essential aspect of shamanism?

My understanding of shamanism, that is, Complete Shamanism, is nothing more or less than complete integration with nature.

10. What is your relationship with community?

Within the bounds of what I think of as my community I am regarded as an elder, and many refer to me as Grandfather or variations of that form of address. I am sought for advice, council, mediation, and humor. I am well cared for and am given many expressions of love. I attempt to live with honor, respect, humility, and love towards all.

Met-a-koo-yen Ay-yay-a-soon.

NINA WOLF

1. What is the focus of your teaching, healing, or ceremonial work?

Those forms traditional and transitional that connect our species and the living Earth and all its life forms to one another and the universe as an interdependent living system. My first teaching and training is through the arts. At this point I'm combining nine-and-a-half-foot kachinas in a Long Dance based on the ancient "Four Mothers" of pre-Incan times. For as long as I've been in practice I have used the mandala and medicine as ceremonial unifying and healing forms for individuals and community. I have used circus, clown, and *koshare* as unifying and blessing tools. I use the synthetic forms "Medicine Wheel," "Blessing Hoops," Four Hoops," "Four Mothers." All were given to me to teach. "Four Mothers" has evolved into its present Long Dance form, as yet undone. So when asked this question I usually reply "spiritual kindergarten." I am available for healing work, counseling, etc., as an elder and an adept.

2. What direction do you see the shamanic community heading toward?

I have not known "shamanic community." I have been living in the U.S. People are divisive and protective. Community based on trust and honoring has not during the last six years been part of my experience.

3. How do you see the dance between tradition and visionary change?

As a dance. Tradition cannot survive unless visionary change alters it to have meaning each generation. Our worlds are changing quickly as we approach the next century. As always, the integrity of the individual adept and the receptivity of the traditionalist determine how easily this dance is done. I am hopeful. Few forms have survived the vagaries of human life as long and as well as this dance.

4. What do you feel are the outstanding ethical abuses, if any, going on in the shamanic community?

Because the modern human often has no community or land base to learn from and ground with, true commitment, concentration, depth of healing are hard to come by. Power can be a commodity like much of contemporary life. Power "with" can be a concept of great change and healing. Humans are a bit dim and often need proof of a material nature upon which to base their belief. Ethical abuse might be quite innocent through ignorance. I'd strongly oppose a Code of Ethics for Shamanic Practice at this moment, or even a Board of Licensing.

5. What are your thoughts about money's role in teaching, ceremonial work, and shamanic service?

I think that traditionally the community the shaman serves supports him or her. It's a good system. Travel money, support money, gifts of value, paraphernalia are all acceptable forms of honoring the shaman's gift to community. Profit does not seem to be appropriate to practice. I don't know of any story or incident I have ever heard of or experienced where personal profit from shamanic services or traditional ceremonies ever benefited either the practitioner, patient, or community.

6. Do you consider yourself a traditionalist?

Yes. However, as a visionary the question is, Traditional to who or what? I've spent a lifetime studying and practicing the traditional forms of two continents—how these forms change and survive—and this is what is of interest to me.

7. What do you feel makes a medicine person a medicine person?

The acquired wisdom of a life, the knowledge and practice and skill of a person freely giving of themselves and their wisdoms to heal and balance individuals and community. Shamanic practice, medicine practice is based on a shared belief system. Where that system has broken, where trust is broken, the practitioner does not produce maximum effect from their effort.

8. How do you feel about the integration of shamanic techniques such as soul retrieval with urban psychological therapy?

Fine, if the practitioner knows what they're doing, and patient and practitioner are both grounded in trust, belief, and community as well as Earth-centered. Otherwise both can get into deep doo-doo. What's a soul retrieval? Lots of people I work with have had this done to them. I think it's scary.

9. Do you think closeness with nature is an essential aspect of shamanism?

Yes. If the shaman lives in the *now* of an urban material culture, the voices necessary to the work have a hard time reaching them.

10. What is your relationship with community?

I live in it, learn from it, am responsible to it. My community is the new villages of Cascadia. My concern is that the best of the wisdom of the traditions of the Old Time be brought in usable form with us into the New. It's an old chicken-and-egg story. Man-animal makes culture the same way trees leaf. If people did not make culture, would our young be born needing so much care? How do we, all of us, assist the young—these young—to grow and fulfill themselves? These children of war have been allowed to reach physical maturity. They have no power—are not conscious of their power. Two decades of greed as a moral guide does not equip people to meet a very demanding future. Respect, as the first peoples understood it, seems to be a key to unlock this one. The concept is not clear to them; the young ones do wonder, however.

Lewis Sawaquat

1. What is the focus of your teaching, healing, or ceremonial work?

Unity/harmony/communication with the world of spirit—"union."

2. What direction do you see the shamanic community heading toward?

Blending with other life directions such as the magical and wiccan paths.

3. How do you see the dance between tradition and visionary change?

As viewed by spirit it is a beautiful dance with past, present, and future all one timeless expression of unfoldment.

4. What do you feel are the outstanding ethical abuses, if any, going on in the shamanic community?

Commercialization leading toward ego and separation rather than harmony and community.

5. What are your thoughts about money's role in teaching, ceremonial work, and shamanic service?

See question #4. Exchange inevitably takes place between teacher and pupil. Except for the very exceptional few, diverting that exchange into money is dangerous.

6. Do you consider yourself a traditionalist?

One half.

7. What do you feel makes a medicine person a medicine person?

Contact with spirit must be a reality. Any amount of acceptance or imitation can never replace it.

8. How do you feel about the integration of shamanic techniques such as soul retrieval with urban psychological therapy?

See question #7. I know nothing as to how it is actually used, but I must admit to being skeptical.

9. Do you think closeness with nature is an essential aspect of shamanism?

With nature as a natural expression of spirit, of course!

10. What is your relationship with community?

An image, an icon, an elder, etc., etc. Personally, however, I guess as a helper.

CHARLA HAWKWIND-HERMANN

1. What is the focus of your teaching, healing, or ceremonial work?

See the biographical sketch [pp. 39–40].

2. What direction do you see the shamanic community heading toward?

Being prepared to rebuild a planet and a people in crisis.

3. How do you see the dance between tradition and visionary change?

These ways must merge and ego must die to let the real work begin.

4. What do you feel are the outstanding ethical abuses, if any, going on in the shamanic community?

Most people who are "abusing" ceremony do not know that they are, because of the teachers, or lack of, available. Those who abuse on purpose simply die a painful death at some point and it is over. I know of over thirty suicides of Rainbows on this path and have documented hundreds that have ended up in mental wards over playing with the "bad guys."

5. What are your thoughts about money's role in teaching, ceremonial work, and shamanic service?

You cannot buy or sell medicine. A healer must still pay the rent, and a ceremonialist has accepted a path of service as a way of life. A balance must come into play. Giveaway on everyone's part is important. That is the law of nature.

6. Do you consider yourself a traditionalist?

Yes.

7. What do you feel makes a medicine person a medicine person?

Lots of work, prayer, tears, suffering, healing, growing up, and getting a grip. The older I get, the quieter I get. But I practice and study everything I can about the dynamics of the energy of earth, water, fire, air.

8. How do you feel about the integration of shamanic techniques such as soul retrieval with urban psychological therapy?

Most medicine men I know must have been shrinks in a past life. I want to know that anyone who thinks they are going to retrieve any part of my soul has been trained and would feel comfortable providing this service for their own mother. I am not very trusting of others' techniques because I have not seen many of them really go through the rigors of traditional training. I think they should stick with dreams.

9. Do you think closeness with nature is an essential aspect of shamanism?

It is inseparable. How can you touch the Earth if you walk on stilts and never taste the blood of life?

10. What is your relationship with community?

I am a clan mother and business manager, a mother, grandmother, wife, and friend to many. I am the gatekeeper to a lodge that provides healing for thousands each year.

[In addition is this quote from an article Charla enclosed with her questionnaire reply:]

> 1993 was a tough year for spiritual controversy. At the point where more people than ever before were asking in a good way for these important Earth teachings and healing rituals, we also found ourselves, as a Rainbow Nation, being blasted as never before.
>
> . . . In late September the pain of this nonsense became more than we could stand. We had prayed and Quested and even danced on it. Still there was this feeling that maybe there was some truth in the fierce accusations of the critics. We had seen some very weird adaptations of the old rituals. We had seen far too many Shaman–scam artists ripping off and raping the women (and yes, even raping some men). We had seen the sale of the cosmic rip-off in some very abusive ways. We had seen vulnerable people taken advantage of, over and over. So again, where would our truth come from? Thus we took it back to the source. With the green energy coming as an affirmation, we drove back to Pine Ridge to share lodge with our Elders in the full of the Blue Moon. We visited the old traditional people who are so often quoted in the "Bad Press" about Rainbows to ask if they were really concerned. We watched the children at the Catholic School who just this year, for the first time, are able to learn their own language and have a lodge in the school grounds. We watched the traditionals struggling to scrape up enough to make a single drum for a family, all the while remembering how easy it is for the Rainbows to go to a gathering and buy these tools with their

Mastercard. The cries of AIM gained some valid points. Maybe it was time to quit!

. . . Yet, again, the answer we sought was our truth, not that of every Rainbow of every circle. . . . With those words deep in our hearts we approached that lodge, ready to come home and bury the Cannunpa and never lead another lodge if that was to be the request of our Elders. Ready to let it all go in honest respect for the Sacredness that might have been violated, we loaded the Cannunpa to present to our Elder. In great humility we crawled into that lodge to pray and find what we should do for Hawkwind and her people. Pain was intense, questions ran deep. Yet in that darkness our light was rekindled as our Elders prayed for our success to continue to keep the work alive for the children of the next seven generations. They prayed for our children as we prayed for theirs. They prayed for unity and harmony and an understanding that we were supported to continue and to grow in these ways.

. . . It is all just a test, they kept telling us. A test to remind us to stay humble. A test to remind us that no one can sell or buy Medicine. It is something earned, prayed for, sung for, drummed for and respected like no other life experience. It is only what we make of it, and is impossible for someone else to judge.

BROOKE MEDICINE EAGLE

1. What is the focus of your teaching, healing, or ceremonial work?

Whether in individual, small, or large group work, the emphasis of my work is on individual personal and spiritual growth that benefits not only that person but echoes positively to serve the whole circle of life.

2. What direction do you see the shamanic community heading toward?

I would hope it is heading toward more regulating of itself, where those who are obviously out of line are spoken to by other members of that community. I would also like to believe that it is creating a (welcome) place for itself in the larger community—for its healing and renewing qualities.

3. How do you see the dance between tradition and visionary change?

I have addressed this before in several ways. The primary thing for me is this: the older, Native ways most important to me are my people's *mystical* spiritual ways—in which Creator spoke to us constantly and in many forms that guided our lives from day to day. This is very different from set religious practice in which the holy books/information were given in the past and are unchangeable. In our mystical practices, the great numinous visions became part of the tribal way, and things that were no longer useful fell away. I believe that without vision and the positive changes it brings, a people become rigid and dead.

5. What are your thoughts about money's role in teaching, ceremonial work, and shamanic service?

Giving support to those who help others spiritually has always been a practice. It certainly was not in the form of workshop fees, but it was expected and necessary. Now we are in a money culture, where support of life takes that form. We can't very easily send a pound of meat through the mail to an elder, or have everyone bring garden vegetables to support a teacher who comes through for the weekend—it doesn't work now. Yet I would like to see the people who support others' healing and spiritual growth rewarded even more. Now, too often a young non-Indian thinks all that is necessary when taking a medicine person's time for hours or days is a bag of tobacco. This is not right. Always, there should be a giveaway that includes food, clothing, ceremonial items (tobacco), and help with housing or furnishing (buffalo robe). Today, the giving of money is what allows the helper/healer to purchase these things for him- or herself. Of all professions, I believe that healing and spiritual guidance are among the most important, and should be valued as such. Why should a medicine man get a bag of tobacco for two days' work with someone who pays his psychiatrist $125 per hour?

6. Do you consider yourself a traditionalist?

The tradition I am interested in is the ancient way of eternal truth as it echoes through our human life. I am less interested in the "tradition" of Native peoples or others which have been developed in the last one hundred years since the white conquerors have influenced and schooled the elders. *I believe the Great Spirit is present in all things and all time, including this very moment—and can communicate with us directly.* I consider this very traditional, yet I do not always follow anyone's "traditional" form.

7. What do you feel makes a medicine person a medicine person?

The ability to create wholeness—be good medicine—for others. I believe any one of us can walk a personal medicine/spiritual path. I would only call those who dedicate themselves to others a "medicine person."

8. How do you feel about the integration of shamanic techniques such as soul retrieval with urban psychological therapy?

If it works, do it! This implies good training, conscious use, and the discernment to know when it will be truly helpful (rather than just groovy).

9. Do you think closeness with nature is an essential aspect of shamanism?

Yes. Shamanism developed from early people's close contact with the Great Spirit alive in Mother Earth and all her children: the finest of the shamans have this aspect to their lives. Those who are modern "apprentices" are handicapped here by their whole culture and milieu, yet the shamanic practice will move them closer to nature if they continue its practice.

10. What is your relationship with community?

At this point, I live in a wilderness retreat, which is very healing for me after all the contact I have with cities and large groups. However, I long for community life—both social and spiritual—and am working to create this for myself and my family. Community seems absolutely essential if we are to find the way to remain on Earth and to live as fully human people.

AXIS

1. What is the focus of your teaching, healing, or ceremonial work?

I used to teach magick but now I do not. I like to help heal people and things and myself. It feels good. My ceremonial work is an in-process evolution of my essential nature and its inherent dream and symbolisms.

2. What direction do you see the shamanic community heading toward?

As always, all directions.

3. How do you see the dance between tradition and visionary change?

Ideally, tradition and change should be lovers, nurturing each other. Seldom is it the case. Tradition is when you've done something in a particular way for a long time—sometimes so long we forget why. Sometimes our beliefs change (heresy); sometimes our world changes. Many sacred traditions these days have become politicized, which severs them from the sacred, for politics enters where love has ended. If it is not about love, it is not sacred. Like the law of inertia, most traditions tend to become restrictive in time. In my work I have piled them on top of each other in the hope of sneaking past any one tunnel reality, into a glimpse of spiritual freedom. To be fair, traditions can be useful—can carry teaching and sacred alignments and can provide a matrix of wholeness for visionary or spiritual work. But far too often the form becomes confused with the essence. Next thing you know, you have a religion on your hands, and religion is not the same as spirituality. I think the whole "tradition versus vision-ary change" dilemma is a mirroring of the tension in the human psyche between the belief systems of the mind and the organic cre-ative process that intersects it.

4. What do you feel are the outstanding ethical abuses, if any, going on in the shamanic community?

I don't know. Racism? Sexism? Sexual abuse? Financial abuse? Gen-eral scurrilous human behavior? How about dogmatism?

5. What are your thoughts about money's role in teaching, ceremonial work, and shamanic service?

Money can often confuse sacred work. It seems, however, to be a necessary part of our world. It should not be so high a fee (for any sacred work) that it keeps people in need from receiving help. In the end, it should be an individual decision for both parties.

6. *Do you consider yourself a traditionalist?*

No.

7. *What do you feel makes a medicine person a medicine person?*

Sacred alignment with the powers of Life. Truthfulness, integrity, capacity.

8. *How do you feel about the integration of shamanic techniques such as soul retrieval with urban psychological therapy?*

I do not have enough experience here to have a useful opinion.

9. *Do you think closeness with nature is an essential aspect of shamanism?*

Yes, but we should expand on what "nature" is. To me, right now, shamanism is a crossing and carrying of awareness between the primal and the complex, with the object of sacred alignment to the truth of being and becoming.

10. *What is your relationship with community?*

To me, my community is everything in the general and everything that touches me in the particular. My relationship is "doing the best I can."

SANDRA INGERMAN

As I have said earlier, I make my services available and people come to see me if they are drawn to my work. It is the community that calls a person a shaman. A shaman doesn't take that title for himself or herself. If you do good work people will come to seek you out.

One important aspect of shamanic healing around the world was the community's participation in healing ceremonies. I know that many shamanic practitioners I meet in this society today are seeking a community that is supportive and promotes work together for the good of the whole. I find many people want to develop community and not practice in such isolation.

I'm an eternal optimist in thinking that at one point there will be shamanic practitioners in hospitals who, three days after a person comes out of surgery, can do a soul retrieval for that person. We're already starting to see more people from medicine and psychology coming to workshops to expand their understanding of healing and to understand what might be lacking in their own processes. I think this is going to be slow, but I've already seen some people moving this work into hospitals in a slow fashion. Some people are moving into this work as an adjunct to psychology. It will depend on whether society will begin to call more on spiritual methods. I personally believe that the only way the planet is going to survive is if people open up to seeing that they are part of a greater whole, and that human beings are not the most powerful creatures on the planet. We're all part of the web; we're part of nature and we have to work with all life forms in order to survive. It's going to be essential to have that spiritual expansion from society for our own survival. I believe that people are going to start turning to spiritual methods more in the mainstream.

MEDICINE HAWK WILBURN

1. What is the focus of your teaching, healing, or ceremonial work?

Self-evolvement; doing spirituality where you are, under the conditions in which you live. My old medicine teacher used to say, "If you can't do it in the median at rush hour, you ain't *spit!*

2. What direction do you see the shamanic community heading toward?

Loggerheads. I really don't think any spiritual community is going to be harmonious any time while I am alive.

3. How do you see the dance between tradition and visionary change?

Traditions came from visionary change.

4. What do you feel are the outstanding ethical abuses, if any, going on in the shamanic community?

Assholes who think they should exclude people on the basis of race or gender.

5. What are your thoughts about money's role in teaching, ceremonial work, and shamanic service?

You get what you pay for. If you don't pay for or barter for something, you don't respect it.

6. Do you consider yourself a traditionalist?

No. Traditions are made by people to be changed by people when necessary.

7. What do you feel makes a medicine person a medicine person?

Intent.

8. How do you feel about the integration of shamanic techniques such as soul retrieval with urban psychological therapy?

Acceptable.

9. Do you think closeness with nature is an essential aspect of shamanism?

No, being at one with your environment is the essential aspect.

10. What is your relationship with community?

The intent of *anyone's* focus should be to help others.

JAMIE SAMS

Jamie Sams, who is of Iroquois and Choctaw descent, is a medicine teacher and a member of the Wolf Clan teaching lodge of the Seneca Nation. A Sante Fe resident, she has been trained in Seneca, Mayan, Aztec, and Choctaw medicine, living and studying with Mayan and Aztec teachers in Mexico during the 1970s. She is the author of Midnight Song: Quest for the Vanished Ones *and co-author with David Carson of* Medicine Cards: The Discovery of Power through the Ways of Animals *and* Sacred Path Cards. *What follows here is an article written by Sams entitled "The Fourth World of Separation."*[*]

In these times of turmoil human beings are being asked to remember their connection to the Creator and to the Earth Mother,

---

[*] This article first appeared in *The Sun*, September 1993. © 1994 by Jamie Sams; used with permission.

145

making those connections strong. Each person's connection to the Great Mystery, to the Earth Mother, to the spirits of their Ancestors, and to their Spiritual Essences holds the key to finding balance. We are being asked to remember that manmade laws or rules are not the laws of the Creator. Human beings tend to forget that no manmade organization is the Source, the only Source is the Great Mystery, the Creator. Every human being must answer to that Source, not to another human being. This truth, though sometimes forgotten, is the way of the Indian Ancestors.

The Fourth World of Separation began some 67,000 years ago with the onslaught of holy wars/over religions, ideas, and separate belief systems created by all four races. Human beings have slaughtered each other in the name of those different beliefs and gods for centuries. We are now in the wobble between the Fourth World of Separation and the Fifth World of Peace and Illumination. The ancient prophecies speak of this time very clearly. One prophesy was told by Moses Shongo, a Seneca medicine man who passed into the Spirit World over sixty years ago, who foretold that a twenty-five-year period of cleansing would occur when the Earth Mother would purge the planet. According to his vision, we have nineteen more years of cleansing before we enter the Fifth World of Peace. He said that in these troubled times there would be a group of people who were unloved by their families and that those wounded ones would act out their pain and loss by trying to stop others who wanted peace, harmony, and an end to the separation.

Anyone who is judging another person's vision, dreams, or connection to the Creator does not understand the Indian way. It is not for human beings to "play God." The Great Mystery holds that role for eternity and does a wondrous job of taking care of any wrinkles in the blanket of life. When we point a finger at another there are three pointing back at us. We may or may not like what another is doing, but it is not our place to sit in judgment. The peace we seek can only come from within. If we keep our connections to the Creator and the Earth Mother strong, there is no force in the physical world that can throw us off balance or stop us from following the path that the Creator has given. This Sacred Path is the path of forgiveness, understanding, and peace—not the path of hatred, revenge, fear, bitterness, or making war on another. The truth is always the strongest protection. If we are being truthful, the balance we seek in connection to the Creator is always accessible. When we acknowledge the Creator and turn over our concerns to that Source, we can heal ourselves and continue our spiritual growth with the knowledge that the Maker of All Life will handle it in the way it should be handled. No human being can steal another's spirituality. Spirit exists inside of every living thing and was the first gift of the Great Mystery to all life forms. The Eternal Flame of Love is the Spiritual Essence that the Great Mystery placed at the center of every being. It cannot be stolen, sold, or traded, but it can be lost among petty judgments, woundedness, and pain. The spiritual connection is between the individual and the Creator of All Life. The Great Mystery is available to human beings who are willing to give away the need to hold onto fear and hatred, jealousy, and separation. How any person comes to the Creator is a personal and very sacred path. How any person seeks the blessings of the Earth Mother and spiritual guidance is private. No human being, organization, or manmade rules can change that fact of life.

Those who abuse the gifts they are given, trying to usurp the authority of the Great Mystery, will be held accountable by the Source. It is not the responsibility of any human being to make another wrong for following his or her path or vision. This need to control or inhibit the journey of another is destructive and wastes energy. The Path of Peace is always present. The truth insists that every individual be responsible and accountable for his or her actions, thoughts, and words. Self-righteousness and the need to defend a point of view is a waste of life force. That same life force can be better used to promote good feelings, unity, assistance to those in need, and genuine caring. The ideas of divide and conquer have dominated this Fourth World of Separation, causing great pain to all races worldwide. That legacy of pain was passed to this generation and can only be stopped by an individual. We cannot change society—we can only heal and change ourselves. That is the truth that we are being asked to understand at this time. If we do not stop the conflict within ourselves between bitterness and forgiveness, we will be held accountable for passing that residual hatred and woundedness to our children. I am not willing to do that. Personally, I am not willing to enter any arena that will hurt the next seven generations or waste valuable life force. Others may say or do what they want to and will be held accountable by the Great Mystery. My elders taught me that if a person's heart is pure, the connection to the Great Mystery is strong. The Great Mystery is the only Source any human being is asked to answer to.

As human beings, we are asked to be sober, to heal ourselves, to stand tall and in truth, promoting peace among all people. Living in harmony with All Our Relations does not mean unless they are of a different race or creed, or still wounded and full of hatred, and/or following a crooked trail. Being a force for good in the world is a personal choice. By choosing to allow others their path without judgment we are acknowledging the trust we have in the Great Mystery's Divine Plan. The Earth Mother has sung the song of Spiritual Unity and the Great Mystery has called many whose hearts were open. How that planetary healing happens inside the individual is a part of the mystery of life, and the only question is, Are our personal actions a part of the problem or a part of the solution?

9

Looking Within: Contemplations on Community

Relationship to Community

What is your community? A town? A neighborhood? Like-minded friends? A correspondence network? A spiritual group? A tribe?

What does community mean to you?

If you could create a community, who would you choose to populate it?

What is your basis for choosing?

What do you want from community?

What can you give?

How does one commune with community?

What is your relationship with your neighbors? With your family? With people you live with? Work with? Spiritualize with?

Draw circles. Draw yourself as one, your neighbors as one, your family as one, your housemates as one, your co-workers as one, your friends as one, your spiritual group, clients, and so on as circles. Perhaps color-code the circles for identification. Now arrange them according to your sense of relationships. Put circles within circles, or link some, or put them side by side, or whatever illustrates your perspective of these different relationships. See what the pattern looks like when finished, and what insights this exercise gives.

THE WEB OF LIFE

Imagine life as a web of relationship, all the shining strands interconnected. See yourself as part of this network, with a song to sing, a light to express through your embodiment of life.

Relax, watch, and listen to what moves in this web. Feel its pulsation, the desire of Being to unfold, to become. See the maple tree unfurling its spring leaves. See the seedling pushing upward from the soil. See the butterfly emerging from its cocoon. See the young bird struggling from its egg. See a human embryo, its cells multiplying, specializing, following a blueprint of sacred intelligence. See it grow within the womb and in its right season come forth into the world. See the child that is you growing, learning, reaching out, encountering and mirroring relationship. Look back upon your path of unfolding and look at where your feet now stand. Look deep within for the core of your life's dream. Listen to its song, follow its light. Remember that sacred intelligence guides unfolding for all within right relationship.

COUNCIL FIRE

The council has gathered and you are part of it.

Who is here with you?

Do you feel one among equals? Part of a hierarchy? A gatecrasher?

What mask do you wear when in a group?

Each member of the council speaks.

Are you listening or preparing your own opinions?

What quality is in your listening? Patience? Interest? Endurance? Internal distraction? Reactiveness? Receptivity? Stillness? Encouragement? Reflection?

It comes your turn to speak. You hold the talking stick and give voice to what is in you to say.

Does it come from your heart? Your head? Your feelings about what has been said before you? Your response to the presence of this particular group of listeners? Something you are used to saying? Something "channeled"?

Who are your allies here?

Do you have enemies?

Do you love both?

Someone interrupts you. What is your response?

The fire burns low, the council ends. Are you the same as when it began?

LISTENING TO CRITICISM

You have been walking your spiritual road for many years and are perhaps a teacher, a healer, or a ceremonial leader. You have dedicated your time and energies to this path and to helping others on their spiritual journeys. You have experiences, beliefs, and practices. What happens when your work, or your perspectives, or your relationship to those you help is criticized? If possible, recall some specific time when this has happened.

How do you feel?

What is your response?

Is there a pattern in these criticisms?

Are there useful ways of giving "negative" feedback?

Useful ways of receiving it?

Does it make a difference if you know the person giving it?

Do you ever ask directly for mirroring or perspective?

How open are you to change?

Does change always need to be precipitated by private realizations?

Do you ever admit mistakes?

What is your manner when doing so? Wry? Regretful? Dramatic? Defiant? Self-abasing? Matter-of-fact? Dismissive?

Do you feel betrayed if friends and associates criticize something you've done? Do you continue those friendships and associations?

Does disagreement entrench you more deeply in your own position? Make you doubt your position? Feel embattled?

What criticism have you received that helped you grow? Gain insight? Improve your way of working with your path?

How can teachers, healers, and so on, best interact as a community in terms of differences, debate, and individual concerns?

THE "M" WORD

Picture yourself as a financially comfortable spiritual seeker in modern North America. You buy drums, rattles, smudge herbs, fetishes, personal regalia. You pay for workshops, books, pilgrimages, tapes, therapies, shamanic services. Sometimes these things make you feel good, or energized, or in touch with something powerful. Mostly these feelings are temporary. Real transformation seems elusive. The doors that money opens seem to gently shut again soon after. Why?

Look at the things you've bought.

How often do you use them?

What care are they given?

How much do you really understand their use?

What long-term application have you made of the things learned in workshops and through books?

Where is the current that moves someone on their path?

How deep is your relationship with teachers? With other seekers?

Has the spending of money, the acquiring of objects and experiences, brought spirituality into daily focus and priority? If not, what might?

Imagine yourself to be a healer, medicine person, or spiritual teacher in modern North America. Community is not cohesive. You offer your skills to those who see them as useful. Perhaps you charge a fee of some kind, perhaps you don't. If you do, you invite a judgment not placed on lawyers, dentists, psychologists, priests, or farmers. If you don't, you risk the possibility of poverty or disrespect. Maybe you don't care about the judgment; maybe you accept poverty as going with the territory.

What is right relationship between community and practitioner? Between spirituality and money? Between practitioner and service?

What is the path of mutual support and recognition of need?

How can spiritual teachings and help be made accessible to all and practitioners be taken care of? Is this possible in contemporary capitalistic society?

INTEGRATION

You are a busy person: a parent, a businessperson, a student, a laborer, a caregiver, or whatever. Maybe you are an urbanite, or a townsperson, or a country dweller. Most likely you don't live in a spiritual community. How do you integrate spirituality into daily living? How do you participate in transforming society into a place of well-being for all?

Each moment gives opportunity:

- Each breath: an occasion for centering
- Waiting in lines, for subways and buses, in traffic, in offices: times for meditation or energy clearing of one sort or another
- Meetings, social gatherings, encounters: chances to speak truth and listen with compassion
- Driving, walking, biking, housecleaning, sewing: good times to pray or sing
- Interactions with children: opportunities for emotional maturation, for expressing love, for learning and teaching
- Overloaded schedules: chances to realize priorities, to expand, to practice balance

- Shopping, investing: places to make choices in support of personal and global well-being
- Customer or client interactions: chances to apply principles of right relationship
- Maintenance chores, outdoor tasks: activities that offer communion with the web of life, and remembrance of cycles and of interdependencies within all elements of life
- Meals, "coffee" breaks: times to be grateful and to reconnect with nourishment on all levels

The list can be as long as the day. There is always a way within present moment to integrate spirit with body, with transformative action in a truth of expression that can be appropriate and effective in any circumstance.

Contemplate the opportunities within your own situation. It is a matter of awareness and willingness to change habitual patterns, not of leisure time or a groovy atmosphere.

LOVE

Visualize the universe as a matrix having two aspects: the manifested and the unmanifested, both emanating from cosmic consciousness, the Mind of the Mystery.

The manifested matrix is the world of form in all its dimensions and expressions. The unmanifested is the well of consciousness from which these arise and return, and to which they are joined by consciousness's pervasive nature. The medium through which this matrix moves and lives is love.

Enter the matrix with your awareness. Use the doorway of any form you feel a good and accessible connection to, whether plant, animal, mineral, or something other. From the doorway of form follow relationship's thread to the medicine of that form, to its essence. Abide with that essence as you dissolve beliefs of separation and limitation. Feel what it is that infuses this essence with its impetus toward expression and unfolding. It is love.

Without love there is no call toward participation. Babies deprived of love fail to thrive, often die. Love is what awakens life to fulfill-ment of sacred purpose. As you contemplate the energies that bring essence into form, let yourself expand and extend into the medium of love. Feel the currents of life guided into beauty, into their myriad manifestations of Spirit by this power of love. Feel its strength and vastness. Breathe it; give full awareness to its reality. This is a truth of Spirit that our children need us not to forget.

Conclusion

This book is called Coyote's Council Fire, not Buffalo's or Eagle's or someone else's, because Coyote is a heyoka totem. Coyote is the one who turns things upside down so that what is hidden tumbles out. Coyote is mirror medicine, and this is a book of reflections. Coyote is fool, invoking laughter that disarms, and today's world needs disarming. Coyote is trickster, and this council met without meeting, without even knowing who else was present.

The fire at the center of the circle is the fire of transformation. Coyote, as creator and changer, stirs us to expand vision by feeding this fire. The hotter it gets—the more friction and crisis that comes to the surface—the more surely we must make choices that lead either to useful growth or to simple incineration. The brighter the fire gets—the more shadows and vulnerabilities become visible—the more imperative it becomes to embrace a clarity of truth.

In these times we need to awaken from sleepwalking in illusion, from the confused walking that has taken the world into extreme peril, into denial of sacred life. We need to tap each other on the shoulder and get each other's attention in compellingly compassionate ways. So often we are agitated in ourselves and thence irritated by each other. Those feelings are movement: conflict and heat that can blindly explode into anger or courageously deepen into the refining flame of transformation. The choices faced by individuals on the path of right relationship are the same choices societies and nations face. As individuals learn to move in alignment with Spirit, so will societies and nations. Consciousness is shared—Coyote's mirror medicine—as all life is shared, the waves of change rippling on every shore.

The offered gifts of every moment are awareness, possibility, and infinite spiritual resource. Using these, the truth of wholeness is realizable, can be awakened to. In the long night we can gather at the council fire to listen, understand, and enlarge vision.

When I emerged at dawn from that sweat lodge fourteen years ago on the shore of Lake Michigan, everything was made new. Fears had passed in the dark womb of the lodge. I came into the clear morning like a freshly hatched bird, the path before me marked by the wings of four swans in the summoning light of the world's day.

May we enter a dawn together seeing the newness that is the true strength of continuity. May all races, men and women, awaken to a vision of mutual participation with gratitude for the sacred gifts of life.

PARTICIPATING IN COMMUNITY: RESOURCES FOR HEALING

People exploring Native spirituality who awaken to a need to give something back to the land, and to do something in support of Native people, are often unsure of how to take action. Their desire to make a positive connection is sometimes frustrated by cultural distance or misaligned through an illusory basis of solidarity. It is important to recognize and respond to our web of well-being as a network of sharing that can operate in a real and powerful balance through generosity, mutual support, and good relationship.

There are many ways for the individual to participate in this network through the moment-by-moment choices of daily life. An awareness of reciprocity and right relationship is intrinsic not only to spiritual development but to survival itself. As this is realized, and the spell of greed and fear broken, life can be nourished in fullness.

So often, what passes for usefulness in the public eye is not what is really needed or wanted by the people (or land) supposedly being served. The forced boarding school education of Natives is an obvious example, but more subtle and various forms of this high-handedness are still being foisted on Native communities. One must be careful to seek out organizations or programs that are doing work of true benefit to Native people and to the land.

Here are some questions to ask as you choose the organizations through which to manifest your giveaway:

- Who and what is really served? The organization? The public conscience? A government bureau? People in need? The Earth?
- What percentage of what you give is applied to administrative and other peripheral costs?
- Who is backing the program?
- Does this program have grassroots involvement?
- Whose idea is this project? What is its underlying purpose and intention?
- If it is for Native people, are Natives requesting and running it, and what is their community's response to its work?
- Does this program foster good relationship among all beings? Does it operate from a positive basis?

Listed here are a few possibilities that, from my inquiries, emerged as truly useful places through which to express concerns, caring, and participation in healing.

Adopt-a-Native Elder Program
P.O. Box 3401, Park City, Utah 84060
801-649-0535

The Adopt-a-Native Elder Program exists to create a bridge of hope between Native Americans and non-Native culture. Adoption is a tradition of the Native American people; it does not mean a lifetime commitment, though many friendships develop that will last a lifetime. The program is organized in the Native American spirit of the Giveaway Circle. The Giveaway Circle has a tradition of giving the best that we have. That may be a gift of time, talents or skills, or actual gifts of food and clothing.

Twice each year the program also collects food, blankets, and clothing for delivery directly to the reservation. Those who travel to the reservation do so at their own expense, and the trip usually takes about a week. A special program for children and grandchildren of the elders, who often reside with them during various times of the year, seeks to obtain new or good used clothing for the children. Special education programs for non–Native children explain the Native American culture and their ties to the land. Several classes have adopted an elder, and gifts of love and understanding have circled in both directions.

South and Meso American Indian Information Center
P.O. Box 28703, Oakland, California 94604
510-834-4263

SAIIC's purpose is to promote peace, social justice, and the full participation of Indian people in decision-making processes affecting their lives. To this end SAIIC pursues the following goals:

- To provide information to the people in the United States and the international community about the struggles of South and Meso American Indian people for self-determination, human rights, and protection for the environment
- To facilitate direct communication and cultural and spiritual exchange between Native American people of the continent
- To facilitate access to international resources by providing information and technical assistance to South and Meso American Indian organizations and communities
- To promote and develop the organization of Indian women at the local, national, and international levels and to support their full participation in decision-making processes that affect their lives and the well-being of their children
- To communicate the Indigenous perspective to policy and funding institutions whose work affects Indigenous people

Sacred Hoop of America Resource Exchange
112 Cat Rock Road, Cos Cob, Connecticut 06807-1302
203-622-6525

SHARE is an all-volunteer, nonprofit, nonsectarian organization founded in 1984 to build bridges of understanding and mutual support between the American Indian community and the North American community at large. The organization is supported by a broad grassroots membership, generous private donations, minor grants, and the retail and wholesale of SHARE T-shirts and other merchandise. SHARE sponsors the following programs:

The Children's Cultural Camp restores Native cultural pride, identity, and self-esteem to children at extreme risk and thus increases resiliency to drug and alcohol abuse, premature pregnancy, and suicide.

The Sacred Sites Conservancy rescues sacred spaces from the encroachment of commercial and government activities.

The Native Oral History Program serves the dual purpose of helping to preserve the Native cultures and the languages in which they reside. Audio and video archives of Lakota stories and songs are presently being restored by the Lakota with SHARE's funding.

The Native American Awareness Weeks and Speakers Bureau recommends Native speakers to inspire fund-raising for SHARE while fulfilling the host organization's objectives, such as crafts and traditional lifeways, Earth stewardship, spiritual teachings, and current economic, political, and health conditions within Native American communities.

The Share the Warmth Blanket Program purchases woolen blankets, designed for camping in the Himalayas, at incredible discount. Each twenty-dollar donation delivers a forty-dollar blanket to someone at risk of freezing to death.

Native American Rights Fund
1506 Broadway, Boulder, Colorado 80302
303-447-8760

NARF is a nonprofit legal organization devoted to defending and promoting the legal rights of the Indian people. NARF attorneys, most of whom are Native American, defend tribes who otherwise cannot bear the financial burden of obtaining justice in the courts of the United States. Legal resources are concentrated in five areas: the preservation of tribal existence; the protection of tribal natural resources; the promotion of human rights; the accountability of governments; and the development of Indian law.

NARF grew out of the civil rights struggles of the 1960s and the War on Poverty. The organization is governed by a volunteer board of directors composed of thirteen Native Americans from different tribes throughout the country and with a variety of expertise in Native American matters.

Rainforest Action Network
450 Sansome, Suite 700, San Francisco, California 94111
415-398-4404

The Rainforest Action Network (RAN) is a nonprofit activist organization working to save the world's rain forests and support the rights of Indigenous peoples. Begun in 1985, RAN works internationally in cooperation with other environmental and human rights organizations on major campaigns to protect rain forests. RAN's methods include:

- Negotiation to resolve problems
- Public pressure
- Direct action, such as letter-writing campaigns, boycotts, consumer action campaigns, demonstrations, and selective bans
- Grassroots organizing in the United States
- Building coalitions and collaborating with other environmental, scientific, and grassroots groups
- Organizing conferences and seminars
- Conducting research
- Supporting economic alternatives to deforestation
- Facilitating communication between U.S. and Third World organizers
- Spearheading public education and media outreach projects and small grants to groups in tropical countries

RAN works with environmental and human rights groups in sixty countries, sharing information and coordinating the North American role in worldwide campaigns.

Arctic to Amazonia Alliance
P.O. Box 73, Strafford, Vermont 05702
802-765-4337

Arctic to Amazonia Alliance is a charitable, nonprofit, educational, cultural, and research organization devoted to constructive and non-violent social change at the grassroots level. The Alliance specializes in designing initiatives that build bridges between Indigenous and non-Indigenous people, and that incorporate Indigenous thinking into contemporary problem solving such as the use of oral history in public schools as a means of combating cultural stereotypes; the teaching of consensus-building procedures in conflict resolution; and the application of Indigenous technology to environmental stewardship.

The Alliance is a network of skilled Indigenous and non-Indigenous individuals—teachers, activists, environmentalists, artists, trainers, and others—who are committed to collaborative approaches. The capabilities of the Alliance can be summarized as direct community assistance, policy research and advising, and coalition building and campaigning.

For Further Reading

The Spirit of Place
A Workbook for Sacred Alignment
Loren Cruden • ISBN 0-89281-511-6 • $16.95 pb

Arranged to follow the progress of the seasons, *The Spirit of Place* offers ideas and ceremonies for developing a spirituality that is indigenous to the land and accessible to all of us. Visualizations and prayers focus the mind; acknowledging totems and allies strengthens the will; meditation centers the spirit; and heightened intuition opens the heart to change and acceptance. Essential companions in these practices are the plants, animals, and minerals sharing our world. Useful for people at all levels of experience, *The Spirit of Place* can be returned to again and again, to challenge and inspire; its wisdom leads us to a greater spiritual attunement with the cycles of our living Earth.

Sacred Earth
The Spiritual Landscape of Native America
Arthur Versluis • ISBN 0-89281-352-0 • $10.95 pb

"Versluis offers a much-needed understanding of Native American religion. Through discussion of how the religions of Native Americans compare to traditional religions, he finds ground for a common spirituality. While contemporary society emphasizes ecology, Versluis points out that Native Americans always had a love and respect for the environment and a recognition of the spiritual qualities of nature. This book is necessary reading for those seeking a greater understanding of Native American spirituality." **Library Journal**

Manitou

The Sacred Landscape of
New England's Native Civilization

James W. Mavor, Jr. and Byron E. Dix
0-89281-078-5 • $18.95 pb
150 Illustrations

Byron Dix and James Mavor tell the fascinating story of the discovery and exploration of hundreds of stone structures throughout New England that are believed to be ancient Native ritual and calendar sites.

"... among the few innovative advances in the field of New England archaeology in recent years ... looks at a class of data which are ordinarily overlooked by both prehistorians and historians, and begins to fit them into a new paradigm ... sensitively written and generally well-supported by documentary and excavational evidence."
Massachusetts Archaeological Society

"Manitou's ground-breaking treatment, handsomely illustrated with photos, maps, and line drawings, will unquestionably propel the emerging field of American geomancy considerably forward. A contemplation of the manitou worldview, presented here with excellence and mature excitement, yields a radically different appraisal of a fundamental aspect of our national history and geography, while suggesting new land–use and conservation parameters for the future."
Yoga Journal

Painting the Dream

The Visionary Art of Navajo Painter
David Chethlahe Paladin

ISBN 0-89281-440-3 • $24.95 pb • 35 full-color art reproductions

Praised by critics and sought by collectors, the art of David Paladin (1926-1984) is rich with the symbolism of Native traditions.

"The leading Navajo modern artist." **Newsweek**

"A well-balanced monograph of a man and artist who led an astonishing life...a fascinating book." **New Mexico Magazine**

Navajo and Tibetan Sacred Wisdom

Sacred Wisdom

The Circle of the Spirit

Peter Gold • 0-89281-411-X • $29.95 pb
175 color and black-and-white illustrations

The similarity between Navajos and Tibetans has often been noted by scholars: the mandala sand paintings common to both cultures, their profound ideas about matter and spirit, as well as the uncanny physical resemblance between the two peoples. In *Navajo and Tibetan Sacred Wisdom*, anthropologist Peter Gold draws extensive parallels between the two cultures' creation myths, cosmology, geomancy, psychology, visionary arts, and healing and initiation rituals.

"A bold and exciting exploration, showing many astonishing parallels between these precious and imperiled traditions, from which our own world-weary western culture has so much to learn." **Peter Matthiessen**
Author of The Snow Leopard *and* Indian Country

"At long last the mighty indigenous traditions of Navajo and Tibetan are juxtaposed, to let their powerful teachings reinforce each other and resound together. A beautiful, wise book." **Joanna Macy**
Author of World as Lover, World as Self

These and other Inner Traditions titles are available at many fine bookstores or, to order directly from the publisher, send a check or money order for the total amount, payable to Inner Traditions, plus $3.00 shipping and handling for the first book and $1.00 for each additional book to:

Inner Traditions
One Park Street
Rochester, VT 05767

Be sure to request a free catalog.